SANTA FE

A Local's Enchanting Journey Through the City Different

TRAVEL SERIES

KIMBERLY BURK CORDOVA

To the resilient Indigenous People of New Mexico, whose enduring spirit and cultural heritage are woven into the heart of Santa Fe. This book is dedicated to honoring not only your legacy but also the vibrant community of artists, storytellers, and visionaries who contribute to Santa Fe's distinctive charm and profound cultural landscape. May these pages serve as a celebration of the rich traditions, diverse voices, and timeless beauty that make Santa Fe a truly remarkable place and inspire us all to preserve and protect this heritage.

"Santa Fe is an inspirational place. Its geographical beauty, sheer mountains, visceral colors, pure air, and unending sky make it a magical place for me."

— D.H. LAWRENCE, RENOWNED ENGLISH WRITER

CONTENTS

AUTHOR'S NOTE

Welcome to *Santa Fe: A Local's Enchanting Journey Through the City Different*. This book, a revised and expanded version of Santa Fe Uncovered: A Local's Insight into the Heart of New Mexico, is a significant milestone for me. It's the first book I ever wrote, inspired by my love for this enchanting city and a desire to share its unique beauty. Santa Fe, with its rich history, vibrant culture, and stunning landscapes, is a city like no other, and I've endeavored to capture its essence for both visitors and residents.

Since the initial publication, I've been deeply honored and immensely grateful for the valuable feedback you, my readers, have shared. Your insights were not just helpful, but they were the cornerstone of this revised edition. I wanted this new version to be a reflection not just of my voice but also of the voices of those who reached out with their suggestions and experiences. I've expanded the guide with personal stories, insider tips, and a deeper dive into the hidden gems that make Santa Fe so unique.

This rewrite not only represents the evolution of this guide but also my personal growth as a writer. It's a testament to the dedication and the love I have for Santa Fe and my gratitude to all of you who have been a part of this journey. As I've grown, so has this guide, and I hope you'll feel the passion and commitment that went into this version. I genuinely hope these pages enhance your experiences and make your journey through Santa Fe as memorable as mine has been.

Thank you for joining me on this adventure. May your time in Santa Fe be filled with unforgettable moments and endless enchantment. I encourage you to explore Santa Fe with an open heart and a curious mind, and I look forward to hearing about your experiences with the guide and the city.

Warm regards,

Kimberly Burk Cordova

INTRODUCTION

Overview of Santa Fe's Unique Charm

Perched high in the New Mexican desert, Santa Fe is not just a destination but an enchanting experience—a place where history, art, and natural beauty intertwine in captivating ways. Known as "The City Different," Santa Fe beckons visitors to immerse themselves in its unique charm and cultural richness. Here, the spirits of Native American, Spanish, and Anglo heritage converge, shaping the city's vibrant identity and creating a harmonious blend of tradition and innovation. This fusion of cultures, palpable in everything from Santa Fe's iconic adobe architecture to the artistic expressions that spill onto the streets, walls, and landscapes, is a unique aspect that will surely pique your interest.

Santa Fe's beauty is more than skin-deep. Its visual appeal extends beyond the renowned Pueblo-style architecture to an aesthetic that weaves the city's past and present together. The vast, high-desert skies, the rugged mountain backdrops, and the distinct palette of colors—all bathed in the golden glow of the Southwestern sun—set the stage for a place that feels both ancient and alive. Visitors here can wander among historic landmarks that whisper stories from centuries ago and explore vibrant neighborhoods teeming with galleries, boutiques, and eateries, each reflecting the city's soul and character.

A Glimpse into History

As one of the oldest cities in the United States, Santa Fe's history predates the arrival of European settlers. Established as the Spanish "Kingdom of New Mexico" capital in 1610, the city has witnessed centuries of cultural exchange and transformation. At its heart lies the historic Plaza, a gathering place that has borne witness to generations of trade, celebration, and tradition. It served as a pivotal hub for the Santa Fe Trail, connecting traders and travelers across vast distances in the 19th century. Today, Santa Fe's historic architecture stands as a tribute to these layers of history, inviting visitors to step back in time and walk in the footsteps of those who shaped its story.

What to Expect from This Guide

This travel guide is not just a collection of information but your personal gateway into the heart of Santa Fe. Inside, you'll find everything you need to explore this city like a local, whether you're uncovering hidden gems, savoring world-renowned Southwestern cuisine, or immersing yourself in the city's thriving art and music scenes. We'll take you beyond the usual tourist spots and into the places that make Santa Fe truly unforgettable—from quiet, tucked-away courtyards and bustling local markets to scenic outdoor trails and historic sites steeped in stories.

Santa Fe is a treasure trove for every kind of traveler. For art lovers, we've curated a journey through the city's iconic galleries, world-class museums, and lively art markets. History enthusiasts will appreciate the guide's exploration of Santa Fe's historical landmarks, while outdoor adventurers will discover a landscape of stunning beauty and endless opportunities for hiking, skiing, and stargazing. Families, too, will find suggestions for engaging activities that bring Santa Fe's magic to life for visitors of all ages. This diverse range of activities is sure to excite and entice you to experience Santa Fe.

Whether you're visiting for a weekend or planning an extended stay, this guide provides insights into Santa Fe's seasonal experiences, from the festive energy of summer concerts under the stars to the warm glow of farolitos lighting the way through winter nights. We'll also delve into practical tips on transportation, accommodations, dining, and more, ensuring you navigate the city with ease and confidence, making you feel prepared for your journey.

Embark on Your Journey

Santa Fe is a city where the past and the present dance together, and every street holds a story waiting to be discovered. From dawn until dusk, there is a rhythm and energy here that is both grounding and inspiring. So, let this guide be your companion, whether you're wandering its historic streets, sampling its flavors, or simply soaking in its natural beauty. Embrace the spirit of "The City Different," where each moment is an opportunity to create memories that will linger long after your journey ends.

Welcome to Santa Fe, where time seems to stand still, and every corner holds the promise of something new to uncover. The best times to visit are in the spring and fall when mild weather and fewer crowds make it the perfect season to explore Santa Fe's hidden treasures.

CHAPTER 1

ESSENTIAL INFORMATION – UNDERSTANDING SANTA FE'S LOCAL CUSTOMS AND PRACTICAL TIPS

TIME ZONE AND LOCAL CUSTOMS

Time Zone

Santa Fe, New Mexico, operates on Mountain Standard Time (MST) and observes daylight saving time from the second Sunday in March to the first Sunday in November. Be sure to check the local time and adjust your schedule accordingly to make the most of your visit.

Local Customs

- **Respect for Tradition**: Santa Fe's deep cultural heritage is cherished and celebrated throughout the year. Whether you're attending an event like the Fiesta de Santa Fe, witnessing the burning of Zozobra, or browsing through the Santa Fe Indian Market, it's essential to approach each experience with an open mind and respect for the community. Participating in local customs can be a profound way to connect with the city and its people.

- **Cultural Etiquette**: If you plan to visit any of the Native American pueblos or attend cultural ceremonies, be sure to follow all provided guidelines. Many pueblos have rules about photography, particularly in sacred areas. Always ask for permission before taking photos, and be mindful of areas that may be restricted.
- **Casual and Relaxed Atmosphere**: Santa Fe has a relaxed and welcoming atmosphere, and locals encourage visitors to dress comfortably. Whether you're exploring art galleries, attending cultural events, or hiking in the surrounding areas, casual attire is the norm. Embrace the slower pace and enjoy the laid-back ambiance that makes this city so refreshing.

ALTITUDE AND WEATHER CONSIDERATIONS

Acclimating to the Altitude

Sitting at over 7,000 feet above sea level, Santa Fe's altitude can be a new experience for many visitors. It's wise to take it easy during your first day or two, stay hydrated, and limit alcohol intake to help your body adjust. If you're planning physical activities, consider spacing them out over a few days to allow for acclimatization.

Weather Patterns

Local Weather Patterns and Best Time to Visit: Santa Fe experiences four distinct seasons, each offering unique experiences. Summers are warm and sunny, perfect for outdoor activities, while winters bring colder temperatures and occasional snow, transforming the landscape. Spring and fall are ideal times to visit, with mild weather, fewer crowds, and vibrant scenery. Regardless of the season, it's a good idea to bring layers, as temperatures can vary throughout the day. The best time to visit Santa Fe is during the spring and fall when the weather is mild and the city is less crowded.

EMERGENCY CONTACTS

Local Authorities

In any emergency, dial 911 to reach police, fire, or medical services in Santa Fe.

Hospitals

- **Christus St. Vincent Regional Medical Center**: Located at 455 St. Michael's Drive, this full-service hospital provides 24/7 emergency care.
- **Presbyterian Santa Fe Medical Center**: Located at 4801 Beckner Road, this facility also offers comprehensive medical services and emergency care.

Pharmacies and Urgent Care

For non-emergency needs, you'll find several pharmacies and urgent care centers throughout the city, with most open seven days a week. Major pharmacy chains are available, as well as locally-owned options for a more personalized experience.

TRANSPORTATION AND PARKING

Public Transit Options

Santa Fe offers a reliable public transit system through Santa Fe Trails, with routes covering key areas of the city. Day passes are available for convenient travel, and the New Mexico Rail Runner Express offers a scenic train route to Albuquerque, ideal for a day trip.

Parking Tips

Parking is generally available in the downtown area, but it can fill up quickly during peak tourist seasons. Public parking lots are located near the Plaza and Canyon Road, and several apps are available to help you locate real-time parking availability. Many lots offer hourly rates, and some hotels provide shuttle services to key attractions.

TIPPING NORMS

Restaurants, Cafes, and Bars

Tipping is customary in Santa Fe, with 20-25% being standard at restaurants, cafes, and bars. Many cafes have tip jars if you order at the counter. For table service, gratuities are often expected and appreciated, especially for quality service.

Hotels and Spas

Hotel staff, including housekeeping and bellhops, typically receive tips for their services. A $2-$5 tip per night for housekeeping and $1-$2 per bag for bellhops is common. If you're enjoying spa services, a 15-20% gratuity is appreciated, with an extra tip for exceptional service.

Transportation Services

If you're using taxis, rideshare services, or airport shuttles, tipping is a standard practice. Round up your fare or add 15-20%, depending on the service level. For private tours or guided excursions, $5-$10 per person is customary, especially if your guide offers personalized insights or assistance.

ADDITIONAL LOCAL INSIGHTS

Unique Local Laws and Customs

Santa Fe has its own local laws and customs to be mindful of. Public consumption of alcohol is restricted, and some items, such as eagle feathers, may be illegal to purchase unless specifically authorized. Be sure to adhere to noise ordinances, especially when visiting residential neighborhoods.

ENVIRONMENTAL RESPECT

Santa Fe's high desert environment is both delicate and precious. When hiking, stick to marked trails to avoid damaging fragile ecosystems. Avoid littering and respect the local wildlife by observing from a distance. Remember that preserving the natural beauty of Santa Fe ensures that future visitors can enjoy it just as much as you do.

CHAPTER 2

WEATHER AND CLIMATE – WHAT TO EXPECT EACH SEASON AND HOW TO PREPARE

SPRING (MARCH TO MAY)

Weather: Santa Fe's spring is a time of mild beauty, with daytime temperatures ranging from 50°F to 70°F. Nights can be quite cool, averaging between 30°F and 40°F, adding a touch of crispness to the air.

What to Pack:

- **Layers**: Light jackets, sweaters, and long sleeves are essential for adapting to spring's fluctuating temperatures.
- **Comfortable Shoes**: These are not just a suggestion but a necessity for exploring the outdoor attractions and historical sites that Santa Fe has to offer. Get ready to step into adventure!
- **Umbrella**: While spring is generally dry, occasional showers may occur.

Seasonal Highlights:

- **Activities**: Take advantage of the blooming wildflowers and enjoy springtime hikes or visit the Santa Fe Botanical Garden.
- **Events**: Spring is a wonderful time for art festivals and gallery events. Fewer crowds make it perfect for exploring the historic sites.

SUMMER (JUNE TO AUGUST)

Weather: Summers are warm, with daytime highs from 80°F to 90°F. Nights are cooler, averaging around 50°F to 60°F.

What to Pack:

- **Light, Breathable Clothing**: Bring comfortable clothing for daytime activities, like shorts, t-shirts, and sundresses.
- **Sun Protection**: Your safety and comfort are our priority. Pack high-SPF sunscreen, sunglasses, and a wide-brimmed hat to shield yourself from the intense high desert sun.
- **Water Bottle**: Stay hydrated as you explore outdoor attractions like hiking trails and the Rio Grande.

Seasonal Highlights:

- **Activities**: Summer is ideal for outdoor activities, including hiking, rafting, and farmers' markets.
- **Events**: Don't miss the Santa Fe Opera or local markets showcasing crafts and fresh produce.

FALL (SEPTEMBER TO NOVEMBER)

Weather: Fall temperatures range from 60°F to 70°F during the day, with cooler nights around 30°F to 40°F.

What to Pack:

- **Layers**: Bring a mix of sweaters, jackets, and long sleeves to handle changing temperatures.
- **Comfortable Walking Shoes**: Perfect for attending festivals and enjoying scenic autumn walks.
- **Camera**: Capture the breathtaking fall foliage, especially along the Aspen Vista Trail.

Seasonal Highlights:

- **Activities**: Fall foliage is stunning in Santa Fe, particularly on the scenic mountain trails.
- **Events**: Enjoy the Santa Fe Wine & Chile Fiesta, fall art tours, and local harvest festivals.

WINTER (DECEMBER TO FEBRUARY)

Weather: Winter days range from 30°F to 50°F, with frigid nights averaging between 10°F and 20°F.

What to Pack:

- **Warm Layers**: Heavy coats, thermal layers, gloves, and hats are necessary for chilly days and nights.
- **Winter Boots**: Ideal for snowy or icy conditions, particularly if you plan to ski or snowshoe.
- **Indoor Activities**: Bring books or tablets for cozy days by the fire or enjoy Santa Fe's many indoor attractions, such as the Georgia O'Keeffe Museum, the New Mexico Museum of Art, or the Museum of International Folk Art.

SEASONAL HIGHLIGHTS:

- **Activities**: Winter is the perfect season for skiing, snowshoeing, and enjoying holiday events like the Canyon Road Farolito Walk.
- **Events**: Experience Santa Fe's festive side with holiday lights and seasonal performances.

GENERAL PACKING TIPS

- **Comfortable Walking Shoes**: Santa Fe's historic streets and outdoor trails are best enjoyed on foot. Bring durable shoes to navigate the city's unique, walkable terrain, which includes cobblestone streets, uneven sidewalks, and some steep inclines.
- **Sun Protection**: The high-altitude sun is strong throughout the year. Don't forget sunscreen, sunglasses, and a hat for added protection.
- **Reusable Water Bottle**: A must-have to stay hydrated in Santa Fe's dry climate.
- **Camera or Smartphone**: Be ready to capture Santa Fe's stunning landscapes, historic architecture, and vibrant cultural scenes.

SPECIAL EVENT TIPS

- **Festive Attire**: If you plan to attend the Santa Fe Fiesta or other celebrations, consider packing festive clothing such as a colorful dress or a traditional Pueblo shirt to embrace the local spirit. When attending events with Native American influences, wear respectful attire that honors the traditions you're experiencing, such as a modest dress or a shirt with long sleeves.

- **Cultural Sensitivity**: When attending events with Native American influences, wear respectful attire that honors the traditions you're experiencing.

Understanding Santa Fe's seasonal weather variations and packing accordingly ensures a comfortable and enjoyable visit. Whether strolling through the Plaza in spring or enjoying winter festivities, adapting your wardrobe and activities to the season enhances your overall experience in "The City Different."

CHAPTER 3

GETTING AROUND SANTA FE – TRANSPORTATION OPTIONS AND LOCAL TIPS

TRANSPORTATION OPTIONS

Flights: Santa Fe Regional Airport (SAF)

Santa Fe has a regional airport serving limited domestic flights. However, many travelers prefer flying into Albuquerque International Sunport (ABQ), approximately an hour's drive from Santa Fe. Airlines such as American, Delta, and Southwest operate regular flights to and from these airports. Shuttle services are available from Albuquerque, with companies like Sandia Shuttle and Groome Transportation offering convenient, scheduled rides directly to Santa Fe. Reservations are recommended, especially during peak travel seasons.

Trains: Rail Runner Express

Travel between Santa Fe and Albuquerque on the Rail Runner Express, a commuter train that offers a scenic and cost-effective journey. The Santa Fe Depot, located in the Railyard District, is within walking distance of downtown attractions. Check the Rail Runner Express website for schedules, fares, and passes—special deals are often available for families and seniors.

Buses

- **Greyhound**: Greyhound provides regional bus services to Santa Fe, connecting with surrounding cities and major hubs.
- **Santa Fe Trails**: Santa Fe's local bus service, Santa Fe Trails, offers comprehensive routes that cover key neighborhoods and attractions. The system is easy to navigate and affordable, making it ideal for tourists staying in the downtown area. Download the Santa Fe Trails app or visit their website to access route maps and schedules.

Biking and Walking

Santa Fe is a pedestrian- and bike-friendly city, with many paths and walkable neighborhoods. Explore by renting a bike from local shops like Mellow Velo or Routes Bicycle Tours, which offer rentals starting at approximately $25 per day. Popular bike trails include the Santa Fe Rail Trail and the River Trail, which are scenic and well-marked. For those on foot, the downtown Plaza, Canyon Road, and Railyard District are must-see areas that are easily navigable, offering unique art galleries, shops, and historical landmarks.

DRIVING AND PARKING TIPS

Driving from Albuquerque

If you're arriving at Albuquerque International Sunport, renting a car allows flexibility for exploring Santa Fe and surrounding areas. The drive via Interstate 25 takes about an hour. Car rental services are available at both airports, but it's wise to book in advance during peak seasons.

Parking in Santa Fe

Downtown parking can be limited, especially near the Plaza and during events. Public lots are available, and street parking is metered in most central areas. Consider using a parking app like ParkMobile to find available spaces and pay for parking on the go.

RIDESHARE AND TAXI SERVICES

Santa Fe is served by popular rideshare services like Uber and Lyft, as well as traditional taxi companies. Rideshares are convenient for short trips, such as heading to Meow Wolf, or for nights out when parking may be difficult to find. Taxis and rideshare services are typically available near major hotels, airports, and the downtown area.

LOCAL PUBLIC TRANSPORTATION DETAILS

Santa Fe Trails: The local bus service covers downtown, neighborhoods, and key attractions with routes that run daily. Bus fares are affordable, and multiple passes are available for extended stays.

Rail Runner Express: This train offers a scenic and relaxing way to travel between Santa Fe and Albuquerque, with stops along the way. Fares are reasonable, and discounts are available for seniors, students, and families.

DRIVING RULES AND RENTAL INFORMATION

Driving Rules: In Santa Fe, as in the rest of the United States, drivers use the right side of the road. Seat belts are required for all passengers, and speed limits are typically posted in miles per hour (mph). Using a mobile phone while driving is only permitted if it's hands-free.

Rental Information: Car rental companies operate at Santa Fe Regional Airport and Albuquerque International Sunport. Book in advance and check age restrictions and requirements, as policies vary.

AIRPORT AND MAJOR STATION INFORMATION

Santa Fe Regional Airport (SAF)

- Location: About 10 miles southwest of downtown Santa Fe.
- Limited commercial flights and general aviation services.
- Ground transportation includes taxis and rental cars.

Albuquerque International Sunport (ABQ)

- Location: Approximately 60 miles south of Santa Fe.
- Services major airlines with domestic and some international flights.
- Ground transportation includes shuttles, taxis, and rental cars.

Santa Fe Depot (Train Station)

- Location: Railyard District, near downtown Santa Fe.
- Rail Runner Express hub, within walking distance of the Plaza.
- Taxis and rideshares are available for onward transportation.

Navigating Santa Fe is easy, with multiple options that allow you to experience the city's charm. Whether you choose to arrive by air, rail, bus, or car, each mode of transportation provides a unique perspective on the city and access to its stunning landscapes and cultural gems.

CHAPTER 4

ACCOMMODATIONS – FINDING YOUR PERFECT STAY, FROM LUXURY TO BUDGET-FRIENDLY

LUXURY HOTELS: PRICE RANGE: $300 - $800 PER NIGHT

Rosewood Inn of the Anasazi - *113 Washington Ave, Santa Fe, NM 87501*

Set in the heart of the Historic District, Rosewood Inn of the Anasazi stands out as a boutique luxury hotel that seamlessly blends Southwestern charm with modern sophistication. Its intimate, art-filled setting, inspired by Native American culture, is a unique feature that sets it apart. Plus, it's just a short walk away from key attractions like the Plaza and the Georgia O'Keeffe Museum.

> *Insider Tip: The inn offers a rotating art collection featuring local artists, ensuring each visit is a unique cultural experience. Don't miss the chance to ask the staff for a mini art tour to delve deeper into the pieces displayed throughout the hotel.*

La Posada de Santa Fe, a Tribute Portfolio Resort & Spa - *330 E Palace Ave, Santa Fe, NM 87501*

This historical resort showcases Santa Fe's rich cultural heritage with adobe-style architecture and lush gardens.

> *Fun Fact: La Posada is famously haunted by Julia Staab, the wife of the hotel's original owner. Guests have reported sightings of her ghost, especially around Room 100. Book a night here if you're intrigued by ghost stories!*

Hotel St. Francis - *210 Don Gaspar Ave, Santa Fe, NM 87501*

Located just steps from the Plaza, Hotel St. Francis exudes old-world charm with Spanish Colonial architecture, historic decor, and serene ambiance. The hotel features a cozy wood-burning fireplace in the lobby and an acclaimed bar, Secreto Lounge, known for its craft cocktails. The hotel's dining options include the Tabla de los Santos, a restaurant that serves a variety of local and international dishes.

> *Fun Fact: Hotel St. Francis, named after Santa Fe's patron saint, exudes a spiritual ambiance that resonates with its historical significance. The staff is always ready to share stories about the hotel's rumored ties to notable local figures, making your stay a journey through time.*

Eldorado Hotel & Spa - *309 W San Francisco St, Santa Fe, NM 87501*

This luxurious hotel offers modern Southwestern elegance, complete with a rooftop pool, award-winning spa, and upscale dining at AGAVE Lounge. The rooftop pool provides a perfect spot to relax and enjoy the stunning Santa Fe skyline, while the spa offers a range of rejuvenating treatments. Located near the Georgia O'Keeffe Museum, it's an ideal choice for art lovers.

Insider Tip: The hotel hosts a summer rooftop sunset concert series featuring local musicians. Guests can relax poolside while enjoying live music and breathtaking sunset views over the city.

FOUR SEASONS RESORT **Rancho Encantado Santa Fe** - *198 State Road 592, Santa Fe, NM 87506*

A secluded luxury retreat surrounded by the Sangre de Cristo Mountains, the Four Seasons Resort Rancho Encantado Santa Fe offers a high-end experience with its casitas, spa, and fine dining with panoramic views.

Insider Tip: The resort offers exclusive outdoor adventures, like guided canyon hikes and sunrise yoga with breathtaking mountain views. Speak with the concierge to arrange these one-of-a-kind experiences.

INN AND SPA at Loretto - *211 Old Santa Fe Trail, Santa Fe, NM 87501*

Near the Historic Plaza, this luxury hotel is inspired by the traditional Taos Pueblo.

> *Fun Fact: The inn is next to the Loretto Chapel, home of the "Miraculous Staircase," an architectural mystery with no visible means of support. It's a must-see for anyone interested in local lore.*

Bishop's Lodge, Auberge Resorts Collection - *1297 Bishop's Lodge Rd, Santa Fe, NM 87501*

Set in a stunning natural landscape, this luxurious resort offers outdoor activities, a spa, and gourmet dining.

> *Fun Fact: This lodge was once a retreat for Archbishop Lamy, one of Santa Fe's most famous historical figures. You can still see remnants of his original chapel on the property.*

BOUTIQUE HOTELS: PRICE RANGE: $200 - $400 PER NIGHT

Inn of the Five Graces - *150 E DeVargas St, Santa Fe, NM 87501*

This opulent inn combines Southwestern and Asian-inspired decor and is a short walk from the Historic Plaza.

> *Fun Fact: The Inn of the Five Graces is frequently ranked as one of the most romantic hotels in the U.S. It's even rumored that celebrities choose this inn for discreet, luxurious getaways.*

El Rey Court - *1862 Cerrillos Rd, Santa Fe, NM 87505*

A mid-century modern gem with a retro vibe, El Rey Court offers a vibrant courtyard and a unique sense of style.

> *Insider Tip*: El Rey Court has its own bar, La Reina, which hosts live music events featuring local bands. This is a hidden gem for guests and locals alike to experience Santa Fe's music scene.

La Fonda on the Plaza - *100 E San Francisco St, Santa Fe, NM 87501*

With its Old World charm, La Fonda blends history with modern amenities.

> *Fun Fact*: La Fonda is said to be one of Santa Fe's most haunted hotels, with stories dating back to the 1800s. Guests have reported encounters with friendly spirits, adding a touch of mystery to their stay.

Pueblo Bonito Bed & Breakfast Inn - *138 W Manhattan Ave, Santa Fe, NM 87501*

A historic bed and breakfast with adobe-style architecture, Pueblo Bonito offers cozy accommodations in a charming, intimate setting. With authentic Kiva fireplaces in each room, it provides a traditional Santa Fe experience that will make you feel welcomed and immersed in the local culture.

> *Insider Tip*: Pueblo Bonito has been around for over 150 years and is locally owned. The innkeepers offer a complimentary walking tour of the surrounding area, sharing lesser-known history and stories about the city's past.

Garrett's Desert Inn - *311 Old Santa Fe Trail, Santa Fe, NM 87501*

Located in downtown Santa Fe, Garrett's Desert Inn provides an affordable boutique experience with a Southwestern flair. The hotel features simple yet charming rooms and is within walking distance of major attractions like the Plaza and the San Miguel Mission.

> *Insider Tip:* This inn is pet-friendly and offers easy access to the Santa Fe River Park, making it an excellent choice for travelers bringing along their furry friends.

MID-RANGE OPTIONS: PRICE RANGE: $150 - $250 PER NIGHT

Drury Plaza Hotel in Santa Fe - *828 Paseo De Peralta, Santa Fe, NM 87501*

Combining historic charm with modern comfort, this hotel features spacious rooms and a rooftop pool.

> *Fun Fact:* The Drury Plaza was built on the site of an old hospital, and some guests claim to feel a comforting yet lingering presence from the building's past. Ghostly legends aside, the rooftop views alone make this hotel worth the stay!

Inn of the Governors - *101 W Alameda St, Santa Fe, NM 87501*

With cozy Southwestern decor and complimentary tea and sherry, this inn offers a charming Santa Fe experience.

> *Insider Tip:* The inn's Del Charro Saloon is a favorite spot for locals and travelers alike. Don't miss their famous green chile cheeseburgers, often hailed as some of the best in the city.

Santa Fe Courtyard by Marriott - *5151 Journal Center Blvd, Albuquerque, NM 87507*

This conveniently located hotel offers well-appointed rooms, an outdoor pool, and a restaurant serving local-inspired dishes. The Courtyard's peaceful atmosphere makes it an excellent choice for travelers seeking comfort with easy access to Santa Fe's main attractions.

Insider Tip: Guests can take advantage of the hotel's complimentary bike rentals to explore the nearby Santa Fe Rail Trail, a scenic route popular with locals and tourists alike.

The Lodge at Santa Fe - *750 N St Francis Dr, Santa Fe, NM 87501*

Featuring traditional adobe-style architecture and Southwestern decor, The Lodge at Santa Fe offers cozy rooms and beautiful mountain views. It also has a theater where guests can enjoy live music and cultural performances celebrating local heritage.

Fun Fact: The hotel's Maria Benitez Theatre hosts seasonal flamenco performances, showcasing the rich Spanish and Native American influences in Santa Fe's arts and culture.

BUDGET-FRIENDLY CHOICES: PRICE RANGE: $80 - $150 PER NIGHT

Santa Fe Sage Inn - *725 Cerrillos Rd, Santa Fe, NM 87505*

With a modern Southwestern flair, this inn offers comfortable rooms, an outdoor pool, and a complimentary shuttle to the Historic Plaza.

Insider Tip: The inn hosts an "Art Walk" in the lobby featuring local artists' work. It's a budget-friendly way to experience Santa Fe's vibrant art scene right where you're staying.

Days Inn by Wyndham Santa Fe, New Mexico - *2900 Cerrillos Rd, Santa Fe, NM 87507*

Days Inn provides clean, affordable accommodations with an outdoor pool.

Insider Tip: This budget-friendly hotel is pet-friendly, so it's a convenient choice for travelers with furry companions. Plus, they often have pet-friendly recommendations for nearby parks and trails.

SILVER SADDLE MOTEL - *2810 Cerrillos Rd, Santa Fe, NM 87507*

This family-owned motel provides affordable accommodations with a vintage, retro Western feel. The Silver Saddle Motel offers clean, comfortable rooms, complimentary breakfast, and personalized service that makes guests feel right at home.

Fun Fact: The motel's "Old West" theme includes unique room decor with cowboy hats and saddles, giving each room a fun, nostalgic vibe that's loved by guests. It's one of the most Instagrammable budget stays in Santa Fe!

King's Rest Court Inn - *1452 Cerrillos Rd, Santa Fe, NM 87505*

An iconic Route 66 motel, King's Rest Court Inn offers simple, budget-friendly accommodations with a touch of Santa Fe flair. The inn has been serving travelers since the 1930s, making it a piece of history itself.

Fun Fact: This motel is known for its unique vintage neon sign, a relic of Santa Fe's past along Route 66. If you're a fan of retro Americana, it's a must-see, and it's especially charming when lit up at night.

These accommodations reflect the diversity of Santa Fe, offering travelers choices that suit every budget and preference. Whether you're looking for luxury, a boutique experience, or budget-friendly comfort, you'll find a place that embodies the beauty and charm of "The City Different."

CHAPTER 5

BUDGETING FOR SANTA FE – HOW TO MAKE THE MOST OF YOUR MONEY

AVERAGE COSTS

Meals

- **Budget**: $10 - $20 per meal at casual eateries, food trucks, and cafes.
  - For a taste of Santa Fe's farm-to-table meals at reasonable prices, **Try** The Santa Fe Farmers' Market Café. Or, if you're in the mood for some local favorite food truck fare, El Chile Tornado serves up delicious and affordable tacos. Both options are sure to keep your budget in check.

Insider Tips:
Many Santa Fe eateries serve portions large enough to share. Consider ordering one plate to split, especially at casual spots, which can be plenty for two people!

Santa Fe's vibrant food truck scene, a weekend staple at the Railyard, offers a variety of affordable culinary delights, from green chile cheeseburgers to fresh tamales. For the latest locations and menus, follow @santafefoodtrucks on Instagram!

- **Mid-Range**: $20 - $50 per meal at mid-range restaurants and cafes.
  - **Try** Tomasita's for classic New Mexican cuisine, or The Shed, a cozy spot near the Plaza known for its famous green chile dishes.

  Insider Tip: Many Santa Fe restaurants host 'locals' nights' with discounted prices or special menus. Don't miss out on these deals at places like Del Charro Saloon on Tuesdays, which are open to everyone, not just locals.

- **Fine Dining**: $50 and above per person for upscale dining experiences.
  - **Try** Geronimo on Canyon Road, where contemporary cuisine meets Southwest charm, or Sazon for a creative take on Mexican fine dining.

  Fun Fact: If you're a fan of green chile, you're in luck! Santa Fe is known for its green chile cheeseburgers, and the New Mexico Tourism Department even created a Green Chile Cheeseburger Trail. Enjoy one of these iconic burgers for $10–$15 at several casual eateries around town.

TRANSPORTATION

- **Public Transit**: Navigating Santa Fe is a breeze with the Santa Fe Trails bus service, which costs just $1 per ride or $2 for a day pass. This affordable and convenient option will help you explore the city with ease, giving you one less thing to worry about.

  Insider Tip: Many popular attractions are easily accessible via the main bus routes, so plan your route to save on transit costs. Plus, Santa Fe Trails buses are free on Saturdays, providing a convenient way to explore the city at no cost!

- **Rideshare/Taxis**: Short rides within the city typically range from $5 to $15.

  Insider Tip: If you're staying in downtown Santa Fe, many hotels offer complimentary shuttle services to nearby attractions like the Plaza and Museum Hill. This can save you on rideshare costs and provide a chance to see the city from a local's perspective.

- **Car Rentals**: Rental car rates start at approximately $40 daily, with companies like Enterprise and Hertz offering competitive rates.

  Insider Tip: Consider booking in advance and checking for discounts through travel apps, especially during peak seasons.

ATTRACTIONS

- **Museums and Galleries**: Admission fees range from $5 to $20.

    Insider Tips: Check for free admission days at the Georgia O'Keeffe Museum or Museum of International Folk Art, which often offer discounts for locals and tourists alike.

    Several Santa Fe museums, including the New Mexico Museum of Art, offer free admission on the first Sunday of each month. Plan your museum visits around these dates to enjoy the city's rich culture for less.

    Santa Fe offers free walking tours of the Plaza area led by local historians. These tours are a great way to learn about the city's rich history and unique architecture, and while tipping the guide is encouraged, it's entirely optional.

- **Historic Sites**: Entrance fees for sites like the Loretto Chapel or San Miguel Mission range from $2 to $10.

    Fun Fact: The San Miguel Mission is one of the oldest churches in the U.S. and offers a unique glimpse into Santa Fe's history.

- **Outdoor Activities**: Hiking and nature walks are generally free.

    Insider Tips: Aspen Vista Trail offer stunning views at no cost.

The Dale Ball Trails, a network of over 20 miles of hiking paths, are free to access and offer beautiful views of the mountains. If you go early in the morning, you might catch a stunning sunrise over the city and surrounding landscapes.

MONEY-SAVING TIPS

Dining

- **Explore Local Markets**: Visit the Santa Fe Farmers' Market (Tuesdays and Saturdays) for fresh produce and local foods. Many vendors sell ready-to-eat items that showcase authentic flavors.
- **Happy Hour Specials**: Restaurants like Cowgirl BBQ and Radish & Rye offer happy hour deals on food and drinks, making it a fun and affordable way to experience the local culinary scene.
- **Picnics**: Pack a lunch with local ingredients and enjoy a picnic at the Santa Fe Plaza or Hyde Memorial State Park, where you can take in scenic views and save on dining costs.

Transportation

- **Use Public Transit**: A day pass on Santa Fe Trails is only $2, offering unlimited rides for the day. This is a great option if you plan to explore multiple areas around town.
- **Walking and Biking**: Santa Fe's compact layout makes it easy to explore on foot or by bike. Check out Routes Bicycle Tours & Rentals for affordable bike rentals to explore trails around the city.
- **Carpool or Rideshare**: If you're traveling with a group, ridesharing can be a cost-effective way to visit nearby destinations like Bandelier National Monument.

Attractions

- **Free Admission Days**: The New Mexico Museum of Art and other museums offer free or discounted admission on certain days. Plan visits around these days to maximize savings.
- **City Passes**: For a savvy way to access multiple museums and historic sites statewide, including several in Santa Fe, consider the New Mexico CulturePass. This pass offers great value and is a smart choice for those looking to make the most of their visit.
- **Outdoor Activities**: Take advantage of Santa Fe's natural beauty with activities like hiking, stargazing, or picnicking. Most trails are free to access, and guides are available for low-cost rentals and gear.

ACCOMMODATIONS

- **Off-Peak Travel**: Book during spring or fall for lower rates at hotels and vacation rentals. You'll also find discounts on flights and activities during these seasons.

- **Book in Advance**: Secure accommodations early for the best rates, especially if you're visiting during popular events. Platforms like Booking.com or Airbnb often have early bird deals.
- **Consider Alternative Accommodations**: Look into vacation rentals or bed and breakfasts, which can offer competitive rates. Staying just outside the city center may provide better deals while still keeping you close to the main attractions.

EVENTS AND FESTIVALS

> *Insider Tip: During the summer, the Santa Fe Bandstand offers free live music on the Plaza several evenings a week. You can bring a blanket, sit back, and enjoy local musicians performing everything from jazz to traditional New Mexican music.*
>
> *Fun Fact: If you're visiting in late September, check out Zozobra, Santa Fe's annual burning of a giant puppet to signify the release of gloom. This unique cultural event has affordable ticket options, and it's a must-see if you're interested in experiencing a truly local tradition.*

Budgeting wisely in Santa Fe lets you enjoy the city's diverse offerings without straining your wallet. Take advantage of local markets, happy hour specials, and budget-friendly transportation options to create memorable experiences that reflect the best of Santa Fe while staying within your financial comfort zone.

CHAPTER 6

CULTURAL QUIRKS AND FUN FACTS – UNIQUE INSIGHTS INTO SANTA FE'S VIBRANT HERITAGE

HISTORICAL MILESTONES

Oldest Capital City

Santa Fe holds the proud title of the oldest capital city in the United States, established by Spanish colonists in 1610. The Plaza, the heart of Santa Fe, has witnessed centuries of celebrations, trade, and change. From hosting Pueblo dances and Catholic ceremonies to military parades and political speeches, it's a place where every stone has a story.

> *Insider Tip: Every year, the Santa Fe Fiesta takes over the Plaza to commemorate the city's reclamation by the Spanish in 1692. It's a blend of religious ceremonies, historical reenactments, and street fairs, complete with colorful parades and traditional music. You can feel history come alive with each step you take.*

Santa Fe Trail

The Santa Fe Trail was a significant trade route in the 19th century, connecting Missouri with Santa Fe. Traders brought fabrics, tools, and other goods, which they exchanged for silver, furs, and mules. This bustling trade route made Santa Fe a melting pot of cultures long before the word "multicultural" was coined.

> **Fun Fact:** *Today, you can still follow parts of the trail that snake through the city. Locals say if you walk the trail at sunset, you can almost hear the echoes of wagon wheels and feel the ghostly presence of traders from another time. It's a truly awe-inspiring experience that will leave you with a sense of wonder.*

Pueblo Revolt of 1680

The Pueblo Revolt is a defining moment in Santa Fe's history. Led by the Pueblo leader Po'pay, this revolt united different Pueblo communities, driving the Spanish settlers out of Santa Fe for twelve years. This spirit of resilience and unity, still resonates deeply in the city today, inspiring a sense of connection and strength.

> **Insider Tip:** *You can see a statue of Po'pay at the New Mexico State Capitol, a tribute to the man who organized the revolt with remarkable ingenuity. Many locals still honor him and the Pueblo Revolt as symbols of resistance and cultural pride.*

CULTURAL QUIRKS

City Different

Santa Fe's nickname, "The City Different," is more than just a marketing slogan. Locals take it to heart, believing that Santa Fe has a soul unlike any other city. There's a strong commitment to preserving the unique mix of Native American, Hispanic, and Anglo cultures that make up its essence, creating a sense of inclusion and shared values.

> **Fun Fact:** *You'll see that even chain stores here conform to the "Santa Fe Style" ordinance. The local Walmart has adobe walls and turquoise accents, blending in with the city's traditional architecture. There's a sense of pride in making sure that even modern conveniences don't disrupt Santa Fe's charm.*

Blue Doors

The tradition of painting doors blue in Santa Fe stems from the belief that blue wards off evil spirits. It's a blend of Native American and Hispanic customs that's become a beloved citywide tradition.

Green Chile Obsession

In Santa Fe, green chile is more than just a food—it's practically a religion. You'll find green chile on everything, from cheeseburgers to pizza, and there's even green chile ice cream! Locals have fierce debates over which restaurant serves the best green chile, and fall is chile roasting season when the smell of roasting peppers fills the air.

> *Insider Tip: If you're here in the fall, visit the Santa Fe Farmers' Market to see fresh green chiles being roasted in giant tumblers. They're addictive, and many locals freeze bags to last them through the winter. If you're new to green chile, start mild—it has a kick!*

NOTABLE LANDMARKS

Palace of the Governors

Constructed in 1610, the Palace of the Governors has served as the seat of government, a military stronghold, and a trading post. Today, it houses a museum, and its portal (covered walkway) is home to Native American artisans selling handmade jewelry and crafts.

Don't miss the opportunity to chat with the artisans. Many have fascinating stories about the history behind their pieces.

One silversmith told me that he learned his craft from his grandfather, who had sold jewelry on the very same spot decades before.

Loretto Chapel's Miraculous Staircase

The Loretto Chapel is best known for its "Miraculous Staircase," which has two complete 360-degree turns with no visible means of support. Legend says that the mysterious carpenter who built it disappeared without accepting any payment, leading some to believe he was St. Joseph himself.

Greg and I were married here, and the staircase added to the magic of that day. The sense of mystery is palpable, and there's something profoundly moving about standing in a place that's held so many secrets and blessings over the years.

Georgia O'Keeffe Museum

Santa Fe is home to the Georgia O'Keeffe Museum, dedicated to the artist who fell in love with New Mexico's landscapes. Her paintings reflect the beauty she found in the desert, mountains, and vast skies. The museum houses the largest collection of O'Keeffe's work in the world, including her iconic flower paintings and stunning landscapes.

The museum offers a self-guided landscape tour that takes you to places that inspired O'Keeffe's work. I did this with Channa, and it's an incredible way to connect with the artist's perspective and feel the inspiration that New Mexico offers.

UNIQUE TRADITIONS AND CELEBRATIONS

Santa Fe Fiesta

Dating back to 1712, the Santa Fe Fiesta is a significant event that celebrates the Spanish reentry to the city. This reentry marked the end of the Pueblo Revolt, a major event in Santa Fe's history. The Fiesta includes parades, traditional music, and dances, and concludes with a mass at the Cathedral Basilica of St. Francis of Assisi. The parades feature colorful floats and traditional costumes, and the music and dances are a vibrant display of the city's cultural heritage.

> **Fun Fact:** One of the most popular events during Fiesta is the burning of Zozobra, a 50-foot-tall puppet also known as "Old Man Gloom." The burning symbolizes letting go of the past year's troubles and is an unforgettable experience.

Zozobra

Held every September, Zozobra is one of Santa Fe's most unique traditions. The giant puppet is filled with slips of paper on which locals have written their worries, which are then symbolically burned away.

The first time I went to Zozobra, I was surprised by how emotional it was. It's not just a giant puppet going up in flames; it's a symbol of letting go of the past year's troubles. The act of burning the puppet is cathartic, and there's an almost tangible sense of renewal in the air. It's an experience that leaves a lasting impression.

Day of the Dead

While not as large as Zozobra, the Day of the Dead is another beloved celebration in Santa Fe, honoring the memory of loved ones. Local altars, or "ofrendas," are set up around the city, adorned with marigolds, candles, and the favorite foods and drinks of the departed. Families gather to remember those who have passed, sharing stories and memories. The city comes alive with vibrant decorations and a sense of communal remembrance during this time.

> *Insider Tip: Head to the Railyard District for the Day of the Dead festivities. You'll find beautiful altars, traditional sugar skulls, and even local artists offering face painting. It's a unique blend of reverence and celebration, and everyone, regardless of their background, is welcome to join in the festivities. It's a great opportunity to experience the rich cultural traditions of Santa Fe.*

LOCAL SUPERSTITIONS AND SYMBOLS

Evil Eye Talismans

Throughout Santa Fe, you'll see blue charms meant to ward off the "mal de ojo," or evil eye. The talismans, often sold in local shops and markets, are thought to protect against negative energy.

I keep a small evil eye charm in my bag, just like many locals. You'll notice the symbol in homes, shops, and even on some of the art pieces around town. If you're interested in one, ask about its significance—the stories vary from vendor to vendor.

SANTOS AND RETABLOS

Santos (carved wooden statues) and retablos (paintings on wood) are religious icons commonly seen in Santa Fe. These pieces, often depicting saints, are handcrafted by local artisans and have deep spiritual significance.

> *Fun Fact:* Every November, Santa Fe hosts the annual Traditional Spanish Market, where you can watch artisans create santos and retablos by hand. It's fascinating to see the skill and devotion that goes into each piece, and you'll leave with a greater appreciation for the city's spiritual roots.

Santa Fe is a city that cherishes its unique heritage, blending centuries-old traditions with a vibrant, modern spirit. From its historic sites to local legends, every street corner has a story waiting to be discovered. Soak it all in, and let the "City Different" reveal its magic to you.

CHAPTER 7

EXPLORING NEIGHBORHOODS – A GUIDE TO SANTA FE'S DISTINCTIVE DISTRICTS

HISTORIC PLAZA DISTRICT: TIMELESS CHARM AND TRADITION

The Historic Plaza District is the beating heart of Santa Fe, a place where ancient adobe walls echo with centuries of history. This area has witnessed everything from grand fiestas to quiet everyday moments, and it remains a vibrant center for locals and visitors alike. When you walk through the Plaza, you're not just sightseeing; you're stepping into the city's soul.

- **The Santa Fe Plaza**, established in 1610, is a living testament to the city's rich history. It has been the central gathering place for over 400 years, surrounded by historic adobe buildings. Here, you can shop, dine, and immerse yourself in Santa Fe's cultural heritage. The local artisans, who set up under the portal of the Palace of the Governors, offer handcrafted jewelry and pottery that narrate their own unique stories.

Insider Tip: If you're here on a weekday morning, you can often catch the Native American artisans as they set up, giving you a chance to chat with them before the crowds arrive. Some artisans have been coming here for generations, and they'll share the stories behind their pieces if you show interest.

Fun Fact: During the annual Fiestas de Santa Fe in September, the Plaza transforms into a lively celebration with parades, music, and the re-enactment of historical events. Don't miss the traditional burning of Zozobra at nearby Fort Marcy Park to kick off the fiesta—a ceremony that has been bringing the community together since 1924.

- **The Cathedral Basilica of St. Francis of Assisi**, built by Archbishop Lamy in 1869, is a peaceful retreat with stunning Romanesque architecture and colorful stained-glass windows. The cathedral, dedicated to St. Francis, the patron saint of animals and ecology, is a reflection of Santa Fe's deep spiritual roots. It is not only a place of worship but also a significant cultural and historical landmark in the city.

One of my fondest memories is when I took Vera to the Cathedral Basilica of St. Francis of Assisi for the first time. She was captivated by the flickering candles and the way the light poured through the stained glass. She affectionately calls it the "Rainbow Church" because of the colorful reflections that fill the space on sunny days. It's one of our favorite quiet spots in the city.

RAILYARD ARTS DISTRICT: FUSION OF HISTORY AND MODERNITY

The Railyard Arts District is a unique blend of Santa Fe's past and present. Once the city's main train depot, the area has evolved into a thriving arts and cultural hub. Here, you'll find contemporary art galleries, performance spaces, and the renowned Santa Fe Farmers' Market. It's a neighborhood that pulsates with creativity and energy, offering a one-of-a-kind experience.

- **Santa Fe Railyard**: Walk through the Railyard on a Saturday morning, and you'll experience the city's famous farmers' market. Local farmers, artisans, and craftspeople gather to sell everything from organic vegetables to handcrafted soaps. The scent of roasting green chile fills the air, and live music often plays, adding to the festive atmosphere.

  Insider Tips: Check out the Railyard's "Last Friday Art Walk," a popular event where galleries stay open late, often serving wine and snacks. This is a great way to experience the local art scene and chat with artists in an informal setting. Participating galleries often feature a variety of art, from traditional Southwestern paintings to contemporary sculptures, providing a diverse and enriching experience for art enthusiasts.

The Railyard is home to the famous Blue Rooster Gallery,
which specializes in Southwestern folk art. You'll find
whimsical sculptures and quirky paintings here—don't be
surprised if you end up buying something, even if you
didn't plan to!

- **Rail Runner Express Train Depot**: This historic depot not only connects Santa Fe to Albuquerque but also serves as a reminder of the city's railway days. The Rail Runner provides an affordable way to explore the region, with scenic views of the desert landscape.

  Insider Tip: Take the Rail Runner to Albuquerque for a day
  trip. The hour-long ride is a peaceful journey through the
  stunning New Mexican desert, with views of the Sandia
  Mountains in the distance. If you're traveling during the
  Balloon Fiesta in October, you might even catch a glimpse
  of hot air balloons dotting the sky.

I've taken Vera on the train several times, and it's become
our little tradition. She loves watching the landscape change
and pressing her face to the window to spot animals.
It's a simple way to enjoy the beauty of New Mexico
with a fresh perspective.

CANYON ROAD: ARTISTIC EXTRAVAGANZA IN NATURE'S EMBRACE

Canyon Road is Santa Fe's artistic heart, a winding street lined with over a hundred galleries, studios, and boutiques. Here, adobe walls, lush gardens, and towering cottonwoods create a beautiful setting that complements the art on display. It's a place where creativity flourishes, and every corner holds something unique.

- **Canyon Road**: Stroll through this historic road and immerse yourself in Santa Fe's vibrant art scene. You'll find galleries featuring everything from traditional Native American pottery to contemporary sculptures. Many artists work on-site, and they're often happy to talk about their process.

> *Insider Tip: Visit in the late afternoon when the sunlight casts a warm glow over the adobe buildings. The Canyon Road galleries often host evening events, and it's the perfect time to enjoy the art in a more intimate setting. Plus, many galleries serve complimentary wine during these events.*
>
> *Fun Fact: Canyon Road is a part of Santa Fe's history dating back to the 1700s when it was a residential area for Spanish settlers. Some galleries occupy homes that are over 200 years old, and you'll notice that the walls are thick—designed to keep homes cool in the summer and warm in the winter.*

- **Teatro Paraguas**: Nestled in an old adobe building on Canyon Road, Teatro Paraguas is a small theater with big talent. They showcase everything from local plays to poetry readings, with an emphasis on bilingual and multicultural performances.

Insider Tip: *Check their schedule for unique offerings like Spanish-language plays or community open mic nights. It's an intimate space that's deeply connected to the local arts scene, and you're likely to rub elbows with the performers afterward.*

Greg and I stumbled upon a poetry reading here one evening. The theater was dimly lit, and the words of the poets filled the room with an electric energy. It was one of those spontaneous Santa Fe moments that remind me why I love this city—it's full of surprises.

BARRIO DE ANALCO HISTORIC DISTRICT: ECHOES OF THE PAST

The Barrio de Analco Historic District is one of the oldest neighborhoods in the United States, originally settled by Tlaxcalan Indians who accompanied the Spanish in the early 1600s. Today, it's a quiet area with adobe homes, historic churches, and a palpable sense of Santa Fe's deep roots.

- **San Miguel Mission**: The San Miguel Mission, built in the early 1600s, is considered the oldest church in the U.S. Its simple adobe walls and modest bell tower make it a humble yet powerful reminder of Santa Fe's early history.

Insider Tip: Don't miss the ancient bell inside, cast in 1356. The church staff will let you ring it if you ask politely—a small thrill, knowing that you're taking part in a tradition that spans centuries.

Fun Fact: Local legend says that the original bell was brought over by Spanish conquistadors and is blessed to protect the mission from harm. During storms, locals say you can hear it ringing on its own, warning of approaching danger.

- **Oldest House Museum**: Located right next to the San Miguel Mission, the Oldest House Museum dates back to the 1640s. Step inside, and you'll find artifacts from the early days of Santa Fe, including tools, pottery, and furnishings that offer a glimpse into the daily lives of the city's first residents.

I brought Vera here one day, and she was fascinated by the tiny rooms and the ancient tools on display. She kept asking, "Did people really live here?" It's a humbling experience that makes you appreciate the simplicity of life back then.

THE SOUTHSIDE: SANTA FE'S EMERGING NEIGHBORHOOD

The Southside is Santa Fe's hidden gem, a neighborhood full of energy, diversity, and local flavor. It's a side of the city that's often overlooked by tourists, but it's beloved by locals for its authentic eateries, cultural centers, and emerging arts scene.

- **Meow Wolf's House of Eternal Return**: This mind-bending art installation is unlike anything you've ever seen. Part immersive art exhibit, part interactive mystery, Meow Wolf's House of Eternal Return takes you on a surreal journey through hidden rooms, secret passages, and fantastical environments. It's a truly unique experience and a must-see in Santa Fe.

Insider Tip: Book your tickets online in advance, as they often sell out. If you go on a weekday, you'll have more time to explore and discover the many hidden details. Kids especially love it, and it's as fun for adults as it is for the little ones!

Fun Fact: Meow Wolf is partly funded by George R.R. Martin, author of Game of Thrones. *He bought the old bowling alley that houses the installation to support local artists, and they've since expanded into multiple cities. But the original in Santa Fe remains a beloved local fixture.*

Exploring Santa Fe's neighborhoods is like peeling back layers of history, art, and culture. From the bustling Plaza to the serene Barrio de Analco, each area has its own rhythm, its own stories, and its own beauty. Take your time wandering these streets, and let yourself get lost in the "City Different."

CHAPTER 8

LOCAL INSIGHTS – DISCOVER SANTA FE'S HIDDEN GEMS AND INSIDER TIPS

Santa Fe is a city full of hidden gems, secret spots, and quirky traditions. Beyond the popular attractions lies a world known only to locals, offering unforgettable experiences that let you feel the heart of the City Different. In this chapter, you'll discover lesser-known treasures, unique activities, and niche places that capture the true essence of Santa Fe.

HIDDEN LOCAL TREASURES AND EXPERIENCES

Ten Thousand Waves

A Japanese-inspired spa nestled in the mountains, offering a unique blend of relaxation and renewal. Locals cherish it for its serene hot tubs and traditional wellness experiences, making it a must-visit for those seeking a one-of-a-kind spa experience.

Insider Tip: Book the "Ichiban" tub for a private soak with stunning views of the surrounding garden. This tub, named after the Japanese word for 'number one', is designed for ultimate relaxation, with its spacious size and strategically placed jets. If you can, visit in winter when snow blankets the surroundings—it's a magical experience.

Fun Fact: Inspired by Japanese onsen, Ten Thousand Waves uses traditional hot-cold therapy. Locals swear by this invigorating contrast, especially during winter.

Kakawa Chocolate House

A unique chocolate house serving historic drinking chocolates made from ancient recipes. It's a go-to spot for Santa Feans looking to indulge their sweet tooth and delve into the city's rich culinary history.

Insider Tip: Order the Aztec Warrior elixir, a spicy chocolate drink based on ancient Mesoamerican recipes. Locals come here during winter to warm up with a rich cup of historic chocolate.

Fun Fact: Kakawa's recipes are researched and recreated from ancient texts. I bring friends here to experience the deep, complex flavors of authentic Mesoamerican chocolate, which adds an extra layer of history to each sip.

The Shed's Blue Corn Enchiladas

A local institution famous for its blue corn enchiladas smothered in chile. For Santa Feans, it's a reliable spot for authentic New Mexican cuisine.

Insider Tip: Order your enchiladas "Christmas-style" for a mix of red and green chile. This unique combination, named after the festive colors of Christmas, offers a delightful contrast of flavors and a true taste of New Mexican cuisine. The prickly pear margarita is also a must-try!

Whenever friends visit, I bring them here for their first taste of true Santa Fe flavors. The cozy, adobe-filled ambiance makes every visit memorable.

Randall Davey Audubon Center

A quiet sanctuary just minutes from downtown, perfect for birdwatching, hiking, and reconnecting with nature.

> *Insider Tip: The Saturday morning bird walks are led by knowledgeable locals who can help you spot rare species. Bring binoculars for the best experience.*
> *Fun Fact: Once the home of artist Randall Davey, the center has a spiritual energy that locals appreciate. It's a place to escape the bustle and reflect in nature.*

CULINARY SECRETS AND UNDERGROUND EXPERIENCES

The Secret Supper Club Scene

The Secret Supper Club Scene is an exclusive, invite-only experience hosted by local chefs. These multi-course meals, held in unique, often hidden locations, bring together Santa Fe's food-loving community in a way that feels uniquely Santa Fean. The exclusivity of these clubs adds a layer of intrigue, making them a must-experience for any foodie in Santa Fe.

> *Insider Tip: These clubs operate through word-of-mouth, so make friends in Santa Fe's foodie scene to get an invitation. You may also find subtle hints on social media.*
> *Fun Fact: Held in settings from private homes to art studios, these supper clubs are a blend of food, art, and community that feel uniquely Santa Fean.*

Coyote Café Rooftop Coyote Hour

A rooftop patio experience where locals gather for sunset cocktails and small plates with a view over the city.

Insider Tip: The Green Chile Margarita is a local favorite, known for its spicy kick and refreshing taste. Coyote Hour is a great time to catch the sunset and enjoy this unique cocktail. Call ahead to check for seasonal availability.
Fun Fact: The Coyote Café helped define Southwestern cuisine in the 1980s.

I love coming here at sunset; it's the perfect way to wind down after a day of exploring.

Santa Fe Spirits' Secret Garden Patio

Known for its small-batch liquors, Santa Fe Spirits has a hidden garden patio that offers a quiet escape for cocktail lovers.

Insider Tip: Order the Atapiño Liqueur, crafted from roasted pinon nuts and local juniper berries, and pair it with a cheese board for a leisurely afternoon.
Fun Fact: Many ingredients are locally sourced, creating a distinctly Santa Fean flavor. This hidden spot is a great place to connect with locals over a drink.

OUTDOOR ADVENTURES AND UNIQUE ACTIVITIES

Sun Mountain Moon Dance

The Sun Mountain Moon Dance is a grassroots gathering on the solstices and equinoxes, where locals hike, drum, and dance under the moon to celebrate the changing seasons. It's not just a celebration, but a beautiful way to connect with Santa Fe's spiritual side and feel spiritually centered. The open, welcoming nature of these gatherings makes them a unique and enriching experience for visitors.

Insider Tips: Arrive early for sunrise or sunset, and bring a small instrument to join in. These gatherings are open, welcoming, and spiritually centered.

This seasonal celebration isn't widely advertised, making it a true local tradition. It's a beautiful way to connect with Santa Fe's spiritual side.

Blue Moon Hikes on Atalaya Mountain

The Blue Moon Hikes on Atalaya Mountain are a local tradition where, during the full moon, locals gather to hike up Atalaya Mountain, enjoying moonlit views of the city from the summit. It's a unique way to experience the city's natural beauty and connect with the local community. The sense of adventure and connection with nature that these hikes offer make them a memorable experience for any visitor.

Insider Tip: Turn off your headlamp during the final ascent to let your eyes adjust to the moonlight. Many locals bring a thermos of hot tea or cocoa for the top.

Fun Fact: The mountain is considered a spiritual site, and some believe hiking it under a full moon offers reflection and insight.

Nambe Falls – The Hidden Oasis

A scenic waterfall located on Nambe Pueblo land, popular among locals for its natural beauty and peaceful atmosphere.

Insider Tip: Visit early to enjoy a quiet picnic and swim in
the pools below the falls. Bring a small offering to honor
the sacredness of the site.

Fun Fact: Nambe Falls holds cultural significance for the
Nambe Pueblo, and locals often come here to reflect and
reconnect with nature.

ARTISTIC AND CULTURAL MUST-VISITS

Shidoni Foundry and Sculpture Garden

A gallery, foundry, and eight-acre sculpture garden where you can
watch live bronze casting and explore outdoor art.

Insider Tip: Bring a picnic and explore the sculptures on a
quiet afternoon. If possible, catch a casting demonstration,
which locals find mesmerizing.

Fun Fact: Shidoni has been a part of Santa Fe's art scene for
over 40 years.

The Opal Room at Jean Cocteau Cinema

A retro-themed bar hidden within the Jean Cocteau Cinema, known for its movie-inspired cocktails and occasional live music.

> *Insider Tip: Try the "Targaryen Torch," a fiery cocktail inspired by* Game of Thrones. *Locals love the cozy, offbeat atmosphere.*
> *Fun Fact: The cinema, owned by George R.R. Martin, sometimes hosts themed events. It's an intimate spot with a vintage vibe that feels like a secret.*

The Lensic Performing Arts Center

The Lensic Performing Arts Center is a historic theater with live performances, indie films, and local events. It's a cultural hub where locals gather for arts experiences, fostering a sense of community and inclusion.

> *Insider Tip: Look out for free community events, especially during the Santa Fe Independent Film Festival. Locals appreciate its ghost stories, too!*
> *Fun Fact: The Lensic is rumored to be haunted; locals enjoy sharing stories of strange tales of ghostly sightings.*

QUIRKY LOCAL SHOPPING AND TASTINGS

Santa Fe Vintage – By Appointment Only

A hidden boutique specializing in authentic vintage Western wear, jewelry, and accessories.

> *Insider Tip: Schedule an appointment for a personal tour with owner Scott Corey, who knows the story behind each piece. Locals come here for unique finds.*
> *Fun Fact: Some items have been worn by movie stars in classic Westerns. This boutique is a hidden treasure trove for collectors and fashion enthusiasts.*

Chocolate Cartel's Secret Tasting Room

An intimate tasting room where locals go for chocolate pairings with New Mexican wines—the perfect spot for an indulgent treat.

> *Insider Tip: Book a private tasting for special occasions. Locals enjoy the unique combinations, like red chile truffles with pinot noir.*
> *Fun Fact: Chocolate Cartel sources cacao directly from small farms, ensuring each truffle is ethically made and bursting with flavor.*

Tesuque Flea Market

An open-air market filled with handmade jewelry, Native American crafts, vintage finds, and more.

> *Insider Tip: Arrive early with cash and be ready to haggle. Many locals come for turquoise jewelry and one-of-a-kind antiques.*
> *Fun Fact: Vendors change weekly, so locals love returning to see what new treasures await. This is one of the best places for authentic, handmade items.*

UNMISSABLE LOCAL EVENTS AND TRADITIONS

El Rancho de las Golondrinas Festivals

A living history museum hosting seasonal festivals that showcase New Mexican crafts, food, and dance.

Insider Tip: Plan to attend the Harvest Festival, when you
can see bread baking in traditional hornos and participate
in hands-on activities.

Fun Fact: Many locals volunteer at Golondrinas, making it a
cherished community tradition. It's an immersive
experience that brings history to life.

El Santuario de Chimayó Pilgrimage

A sacred site with "holy dirt" believed to have healing properties.
Locals make a 30-mile pilgrimage, especially during Easter.

Insider Tip: Visit in the off-season for a more personal
experience. Bring a container to collect some of the holy
dirt, said to have miraculous effects.

Fun Fact: The chapel is filled with crutches and testimonials
left by those who've experienced healing. Locals see the
pilgrimage as a profound spiritual journey.

THESE UNIQUE EXPERIENCES, local secrets, and cherished traditions offer a deeper connection to Santa Fe. From hidden bars and moonlit hikes to artisanal chocolate tastings and historic festivals, each place has a story that adds to the city's charm. By exploring these lesser-known treasures, you'll experience Santa Fe like a local and uncover the true essence of the City Different.

CHAPTER 9

CULINARY DELIGHTS – A FOOD LOVER'S GUIDE TO SANTA FE'S BEST EATS

Santa Fe is a culinary paradise that extends beyond iconic dishes and well-known restaurants. This chapter unveils the city's hidden culinary gems, from cozy bakeries to secret speakeasies. Whether you're looking for kid-friendly spots, fine dining, budget eats, or top-secret locations only locals know about, this guide has you covered.

ICONIC SOUTHWESTERN DISHES AND MUST-TRY CLASSICS

Green and Red Chile

The heart and soul of New Mexican cuisine, green and red chile, is featured in dishes from breakfast burritos to enchiladas. Santa Fe locals recommend ordering your dish "Christmas-style" to sample both flavors. This means your dish will be smothered in both red and green chile, offering a unique and exciting taste that will leave you intrigued and eager to try more.

- **Tia Sophia's** – 210 W San Francisco St, Santa Fe, NM 87501
- **The Shed** – 113½ E Palace Ave, Santa Fe, NM 87501

> *Fun Fact: New Mexico has an official state question: "Red or green?" This question, often asked when ordering New Mexican cuisine, is a nod to the state's Chile obsession. It's not just a question about your chile preference; it's a cultural phenomenon that will immerse you in Santa Fe's culinary culture and make you feel like a part of the local tradition. I love watching visitors ponder their choice; it's a Santa Fe rite of passage!*

Blue Corn Tamales

Blue corn, indigenous to the region, is used in tamales filled with pork, beans, and cheese, then topped with chile. This is a true taste of Santa Fe's indigenous heritage.

- **La Choza** – 905 Alarid St, Santa Fe, NM 87505
- **Café Pasqual's** – 121 Don Gaspar Ave, Santa Fe, NM 87501

> *Kid-Friendly: Blue corn tamales are often milder and make a good choice for kids or those who prefer less spice.*

GREEN CHILE CHEESEBURGER

This New Mexican twist on a classic burger features roasted green chile for an extra kick.

- **Santa Fe Bite** – 311 Old Santa Fe Trail, Santa Fe, NM 87501
- **Shake Foundation** – 631 Cerrillos Rd, Santa Fe, NM 87505

> *Insider Tip: Santa Fe Bite's burger is huge, so come hungry!*
> *Locals say it's the best green chile cheeseburger in town.*

BUDGET-FRIENDLY EATERIES

Tia Sophia's - 210 W San Francisco St, Santa Fe, NM 87501

A local favorite for hearty New Mexican breakfasts and lunches, Tia Sophia's serves up burritos starting at around $10. It's budget-friendly, cozy, and very welcoming.

Dietary Options: Vegetarian-friendly, with options like veggie enchiladas.

> *Kid-Friendly: Casual atmosphere with high chairs available.*
> *Kids love the pancakes and breakfast burritos.*

Counter Culture Café - 930 Baca St, Santa Fe, NM 87505

Known for organic, locally sourced ingredients, Counter Culture offers breakfast and lunch with options under $15.

Dietary Options: Vegan, vegetarian, and gluten-free options like salads and veggie burritos.

> *Fun Fact: Despite being a hidden spot off the beaten path,*
> *locals flock here for fresh, health-conscious meals.*

TUNE-UP CAFÉ - 1115 HICKOX ST, Santa Fe, NM 87505

A funky café serving breakfast and lunch with a blend of Southwestern and Salvadoran dishes. Locals love the huevos yucatecos.

Budget-Friendly: Most meals are under $15, making it a great choice for budget-conscious diners.

> *Insider Tip: The back patio is a hidden gem, shaded by trees, and perfect for a quiet meal.*

It's one of my favorite spots to relax with friends on a sunny day.

FINE DINING AND UPSCALE EXPERIENCES

Sazón - 221 Shelby St, Santa Fe, NM 87501

Led by James Beard Award-winning Chef Fernando Olea, Sazón offers upscale New Mexican cuisine with a focus on mole. Reservations are highly recommended.

How to Get In: Reservations are essential, especially on weekends and during festivals.

Sazón hosted my wedding reception, and it was a night to remember, with exquisite food and a warm, inviting atmosphere.

Geronimo - 724 Canyon Rd, Santa Fe, NM 87501

This historic adobe building on Canyon Road serves globally inspired, upscale dishes with a Southwestern twist.

Recommended Dish: Try the elk tenderloin with green chile for a uniquely Santa Fean experience.

Atmosphere: Intimate and romantic, perfect for a special night out.

The Compound - 653 Canyon Rd, Santa Fe, NM 87501

The Compound combines traditional Southwestern ingredients with international flavors in a fine dining setting. It's an ideal choice for celebrating special occasions.

> *Insider Tip: The truffle mac and cheese is a decadent favorite among locals.*

HIDDEN GEMS – LOCAL SECRETS AND TOP-SECRET SPOTS

El Parasol - 298 Dinosaur Trail, Santa Fe, NM 87508

A no-frills, budget-friendly taco stand known for shredded beef tacos and green chile stew. This is authentic Santa Fe flavor on a budget.

Atmosphere: Casual and unassuming, with a loyal following of regulars. The friendly staff and the smell of freshly made tortillas add to the charm of this local favorite.

> *Fun Fact: Originally a roadside stand, El Parasol has been a local staple since the 1950s.*

Tesuque Village Market - 138 Tesuque Village Rd, Santa Fe, NM 87506

Just outside Santa Fe, this market is beloved by locals for breakfast burritos, fresh pastries, and a casual vibe.

> *Insider Tip: The outdoor patio is perfect for a quiet morning surrounded by Tesuque's scenic beauty.*
> *Fun Fact: Tesuque Village Market is part café, part general store, and it even has a bar. It's a perfect spot to unwind with locals.*

La Reina at El Rey Court - 1862 Cerrillos Rd, Santa Fe, NM 87505

Hidden within the El Rey Court motel, this mezcal bar is a favorite local haunt with a great selection of craft cocktails.

How to Get In: Look for the neon sign at El Rey Court, then head inside and make your way to the bar.

Atmosphere: Low-key and cozy, with a vintage vibe. It's a great spot to sip mezcal and enjoy a quiet night out.

Radish & Rye's Hidden Speakeasy - 505 Cerrillos Rd, Santa Fe, NM 87501

Tucked away within Radish & Rye, this speakeasy serves up craft cocktails with a New Mexican twist.

How to Get In: Ask the hostess for the "hidden bar," and they'll direct you to the secret door.

Atmosphere: Intimate, dimly lit, and perfect for a nightcap. Locals love this spot for its exclusivity and unique drink menu.

The Teahouse on Canyon Road - 821 Canyon Rd, Santa Fe, NM 87501

A cozy café nestled among Canyon Road's art galleries, The Teahouse serves over 150 varieties of tea and healthy, fresh dishes.

> *Insider Tip: The outdoor patio is especially popular in spring and summer. It's a hidden oasis for a quiet meal or refreshing drink after gallery-hopping.*
> *Fun Fact: The Teahouse's extensive tea menu makes it a local favorite for relaxation and unwinding.*

UNIQUE INTERNATIONAL FLAVORS

Jambo Café - 2010 Cerrillos Rd, Santa Fe, NM 87505

An African-Caribbean fusion café, Jambo offers vibrant flavors and award-winning dishes.

Dietary Options: Vegan, vegetarian, and gluten-free options, including the coconut lentil stew.

> *Fun Fact: Chef Ahmed Obo brings a taste of his Kenyan roots to every dish. The jerk chicken is a local favorite.*

Paper Dosa - 551 W Cordova Rd, Santa Fe, NM 87505

A casual spot for South Indian cuisine, Paper Dosa serves dosas, curries, and chutneys in a relaxed setting.

Dietary Options: Gluten-free and vegetarian options dominate the menu.

> *Kid-Friendly: Dosas are a fun choice for kids, and the mild coconut chutney is usually a hit.*

Clafoutis - 333 W Cordova Rd, Santa Fe, NM 87505

Overview: A charming French bakery and café known for croissants, quiche, and French pastries.

> *Insider Tip: Locals rave about the almond croissants and quiche Lorraine. This spot is perfect for a cozy breakfast or lunch.*
> *Fun Fact: Clafoutis imports flour and other ingredients directly from France, lending authenticity to its baked goods.*

CULINARY EVENTS AND FESTIVALS

Santa Fe Farmers' Market - 1607 Paseo De Peralta, Santa Fe, NM 87501

A year-round market featuring local produce, handmade crafts, and prepared foods. It's one of the largest farmers' markets in the U.S.

> *Fun Fact: The Farmers' Market is a Santa Fe staple, drawing in both locals and visitors with fresh green chile, lavender, and local honey.*

Santa Fe Wine & Chile Fiesta

This annual festival celebrates Santa Fe's culinary scene with wine tastings, chef demos, and chile-inspired dishes.

> *Insider Tip: Book early, as tickets sell out fast. Locals love the Grand Tasting event, where you can sample dishes from top chefs and local wineries.*

Santa Fe's food scene offers an incredible variety of flavors, from traditional New Mexican dishes to international cuisine and top-secret local spots. This chapter guides you through the culinary gems only locals know, helping you experience the City Different like a true Santa Fean. Whether you're savoring green chile at a hidden café, enjoying a cocktail in a speakeasy, or strolling through the Farmers' Market, every bite is a journey through Santa Fe's rich and diverse culture.

CHAPTER 10

FUN FOR ALL AGES – ACTIVITIES AND ADVENTURES FOR EVERY GENERATION

Santa Fe is a city where discovery never ends. From toddlers to seniors, the city has something unique for everyone. Here's your guide to exploring Santa Fe with family and friends or solo, filled with insider tips, hidden gems, and places known mainly to locals.

TODDLER-FRIENDLY ACTIVITIES

Santa Fe Children's Museum - 1050 Old Pecos Trail, Santa Fe, NM 87505

The museum features interactive exhibits tailored to young children, including a water play area, a sensory garden, and a life-size adobe playhouse. The water play area is a hit with toddlers, while the sensory garden allows kids to touch and explore different plants. The life-size adobe playhouse is a great way for kids to learn about traditional Santa Fe architecture while having fun.

> *Insider Tip: Arrive in the morning to enjoy quieter play areas and pack snacks for the outdoor picnic space.*

One of my favorite memories with Vera was at the Santa Fe Children's Museum. She was captivated by the mini-adobe village and spent a long time "cooking" imaginary meals for me in the outdoor play kitchen. She loved the sensory garden too. Watching her explore and learn in such an interactive environment is a joy I'll always treasure. And seeing Santa Fe through her eyes is truly magical.

Railyard Park - 740 Cerrillos Rd, Santa Fe, NM 87505

This expansive park is not just for toddlers; it's a community hub. With a playground, splash pad, and wide-open spaces for running, it's a place where families come together. The park also hosts community events that offer family-friendly activities, fostering a sense of togetherness.

> *Insider Tip: In warmer months, bring swimwear for the splash pad, which is always a hit with little ones.*

Harrell House Bug Museum - 433 Paseo de Peralta, Santa Fe, NM 87501

This bug museum features hundreds of live and preserved insects. Kids can marvel at tarantulas and scorpions and even handle certain bugs in a safe, controlled setting.

> *Fun Fact: The museum is also home to reptiles, so there's plenty to keep curious young minds engaged!*

Randall Davey Audubon Center - 1800 Upper Canyon Rd, Santa Fe, NM 87501

A peaceful sanctuary for young explorers, this center offers nature trails, a pollinator garden, and frequent bird sightings. Guided tours are available on weekends.

> *Insider Tip: Bring a small pair of binoculars so toddlers can observe birds and other wildlife up close.*

Santa Fe Botanical Garden - 715 Camino Lejo, Santa Fe, NM 87505

A blend of native plants and interactive exhibits makes the botanical garden a lovely spot for young children. The Children's Garden has engaging sensory elements and plenty of shade.

My granddaughter Vera loves to explore the garden, and it's a wonderful place to introduce children to nature.

El Rancho de las Golondrinas – Living History Museum - 334 Los Pinos Rd, Santa Fe, NM 87507

This museum transports visitors back to the 18th century with costumed interpreters, historic buildings, and farm animals. Kids can try hands-on activities during special events.

> *Insider Tip: The Fall Harvest Festival offers pumpkin picking and cider pressing—a must for families with young children.*

Santa Fe Train Station Miniature Rides - 730 Cerrillos Rd, Santa Fe, NM 87505

On weekends, a small train runs through the Railyard area. The train rides are short, usually lasting about 15 minutes, and are a great way for kids to experience trains up close. The train operates on a regular schedule, with rides available every hour, making it easy to plan your visit.

> *Insider Tip: This mini-train ride is free, but donations are encouraged and help maintain the experience for future visitors.*

TEENAGER EXCITEMENT: THRILLS AND ENTERTAINMENT

Meow Wolf – House of Eternal Return - 1352 Rufina Cir, Santa Fe, NM 87507

Meow Wolf's interactive art exhibit, the House of Eternal Return, is an immersive experience with secret rooms, hidden messages, and a blend of mystery and creativity. The exhibit is designed to engage teens and adults, but younger children can also enjoy the surreal and imaginative installations. However, some areas may be too intense for very young children, so it's best to explore with older kids.

> *Insider Tip*: Bring a flashlight to help uncover hidden details throughout the space.

Santa Fe Climbing Center - 3008 Cielo Ct, Santa Fe, NM 87507

This center offers rock climbing walls for all skill levels, with a focus on safety and instruction. It's a fantastic spot for active.

> *Insider Tip*: They offer *Teen Climb Nights*, where teens can climb in a fun and relaxed environment with music and snacks, all under the careful supervision of trained instructors.

Ghost Tours – Santa Fe's Haunted Past

Teens can enjoy a spooky evening learning about Santa Fe's haunted history on these nighttime tours. Local guides share chilling tales while exploring some of the city's oldest buildings—book with **Santa Fe Ghost and History Tours.**

Our family took this tour one night, and it sparked so much curiosity about local legends. It's educational and entertaining.

Rockin' Rollers Event Arena - 2915 Agua Fria St, Santa Fe, NM 87507

This roller-skating rink is a popular spot for teens. It has themed skate nights, including glow-in-the-dark events, making it an energetic place for a fun night out.

Insider Tip: Friday and Saturday evenings are when the rink is busiest, adding to the fun atmosphere.

Santa Fe Skate Park - 1142 Siler Rd, Santa Fe, NM 87507

Santa Fe's largest skate park is free to the public and a favorite hangout for local teens. It has ramps, bowls, and rails for both beginner and advanced skateboarders.

Fun Fact: The park was designed with significant input from the local skateboarding community, making it a cherished spot for young Santa Feans and a testament to their influence on the city's recreational spaces.

The Alley Santa Fe - 153 Paseo De Peralta, Santa Fe, NM 87501

A classic hangout, The Alley is perfect for an afternoon or evening of bowling. They have arcade games and a snack bar, making it a hit with teens.

Santa Fe Railyard Arts District - 740 Cerrillos Rd, Santa Fe, NM 87505

With art galleries, food trucks, and live performances, the Railyard is a trendy hangout for teens. It's a great spot to soak up Santa Fe's artistic vibe and explore the city's cultural side.

Insider Tip: Visit on Saturday mornings for the Farmers' Market, where local vendors sell snacks and drinks teens will love.

YOUNG ADULT ADVENTURES

Santa Fe Railyard Arts District - 740 Cerrillos Rd, Santa Fe, NM 87505

The Railyard District is packed with contemporary galleries, artisan shops, and coffee spots. It's perfect for exploring Santa Fe's creative side.

> **Fun Fact**: *Many galleries host live music on Friday evenings, which is a fantastic way to experience Santa Fe's arts scene.*

Sunset Hot Air Balloon Ride

A hot air balloon ride provides incredible views of Santa Fe's landscapes, making for a unique and memorable experience. Watch as the sky lights up over the desert. **Santa Fe Balloons** offers sunrise and sunset flights.

> **Insider Tip**: *Dress in layers for cooler morning or evening temperatures.*

Santa Fe Brewing Company Tour - 35 Fire Pl, Santa Fe, NM 87508

Take a behind-the-scenes tour of New Mexico's oldest brewery, complete with tastings. Their outdoor venue, The Bridge, often hosts live music, making it a fun social spot.

I enjoy the relaxed atmosphere at Santa Fe Brewing Company. It's a great spot to unwind and sample unique local brews. I enjoy heading there on Tuesday nights for live trivia with friends!

Ghost Ranch Hiking and Horseback Riding - HC 77, Abiquiu, NM 87510

Explore the landscapes that inspired Georgia O'Keeffe. Ghost Ranch offers hiking and horseback riding trails that reveal New Mexico's stunning desert scenery.

Insider Tip: Don't miss the geology museum on-site, which features dinosaur fossils and local artifacts.

The Tea House on Canyon Road - 821 Canyon Rd, Santa Fe, NM 87501

A charming spot for brunch or an afternoon tea, the Tea House offers an extensive menu of teas, coffee, and locally-sourced dishes. Perfect for a relaxing afternoon after exploring Canyon Road galleries.

Insider Tip: Their tea selection features over 150 varieties!

Jemez Hot Springs (Day Trip) - 040 Abousleman Loop, Jemez Springs, NM 87025

About an hour from Santa Fe, Jemez Hot Springs provides a tranquil escape with natural hot spring pools. It's a perfect way to relax after hiking in the Jemez Mountains.

> *Insider Tip: Try to visit on a weekday to enjoy the springs with fewer crowds.*

Santa Fe Farmers' Market - 1607 Paseo de Peralta, Santa Fe, NM 87501

Young adults will enjoy sampling local foods and finding artisan crafts at this bustling market. The Farmers' Market is lively and filled with local flavors and produce.

It's always a treat to start the morning here with fresh pastries and coffee.

ADULT AND SENIOR SERENITY: RELAXATION AND ENJOYMENT

Ten Thousand Waves Spa - 21 Ten Thousand Waves Way, Santa Fe, NM 87501

A Japanese-inspired spa tucked into the mountains, Ten Thousand Waves offers hot tubs, massages, and a tranquil setting for relaxation.

> *Insider Tip: Book a private tub for a serene, secluded experience, and enjoy green tea in the lounge afterward.*

SANTA FE OPERA - 301 Opera Dr, Santa Fe, NM 87506

The open-air opera house has sweeping views of the surrounding mountains, making for a breathtaking setting to enjoy world-class performances.

> *Insider Tip: Arrive early with a picnic to enjoy dinner before the show while taking in the views.*

Canyon Road Gallery Stroll

Wander down Canyon Road and explore some of the finest art galleries in the Southwest. Many galleries feature artists in residence, offering opportunities to learn more about their work.

> *Insider Tip: Plan a stop at **El Farol**, Santa Fe's oldest bar, for tapas and live music at the end of your stroll.*

Loretto Chapel - 207 Old Santa Fe Trail, Santa Fe, NM 87501

Known for its mysterious staircase, the chapel is a must-see for history and architecture enthusiasts. The serene atmosphere offers a quiet place for reflection.

The Loretto Chapel holds a special place in my heart—as it is where Greg and I exchanged our vows.

Santa Fe Culinary Tours

Explore the rich flavors of Santa Fe with a guided food tour. You'll sample dishes from a variety of local eateries, each highlighting traditional Southwestern ingredients.

> *Fun Fact: Many tours include a stop at **Kakawa Chocolate House** for a tasting of their decadent chocolate elixirs.*

La Posada de Santa Fe Resort & Spa - 330 E Palace Ave, Santa Fe, NM 87501

This luxurious resort offers a peaceful retreat with an on-site spa, lush gardens, and historic adobe architecture. It's a beautiful spot for rest and rejuvenation.

> *Insider Tip: La Posada's spa offers unique treatments inspired by local traditions, like their signature blue corn body scrub.*

La Cieneguilla Petroglyph Site - Santa Fe, NM, accessible from Airport Rd.

This lesser-known site features ancient petroglyphs. It's a quiet place to walk and appreciate Santa Fe's history, away from the crowds.

> *Insider Tip: Bring water and sunscreen, as there is little shade. Early morning visits provide the best lighting for viewing petroglyphs.*

HIDDEN GEMS AND TOP-SECRET SPOTS

Tsankawi Ruins at Bandelier National Monument - NM-4, Los Alamos, NM 87544

A lesser-known area of Bandelier National Monument, Tsankawi features ancient trails, petroglyphs, and cave dwellings. It's a unique hike and a step back into history.

> *Insider Tip: The trails are unpaved and can be steep, so wear sturdy shoes. Morning hikes provide the best lighting for viewing petroglyphs.*

Secret Rooftop Pools at La Fonda on the Plaza - 100 E San Francisco St, Santa Fe, NM 87501

Accessible to guests and hidden from street view, these rooftop pools offer stunning views of downtown Santa Fe and the surrounding mountains.

How to Access: Book a stay at La Fonda to experience this secret oasis and enjoy the poolside bar service for added relaxation.

Tesuque Village Market - 138 Tesuque Village Rd, Santa Fe, NM 87506

This rustic market and café just north of Santa Fe is a favorite among locals for breakfast and lunch. It has a cozy vibe and fresh, homemade dishes.

Insider Tip: Visit for their weekend brunch; the breakfast burritos and pastries are particularly popular.

Kakawa Chocolate House - 1050 Paseo de Peralta, Santa Fe, NM 87501

Known for its historically-inspired chocolate elixirs, Kakawa Chocolate House is a must-visit for chocolate lovers. They offer unique flavors inspired by Mesoamerican, European, and Colonial recipes.

Insider Tip: Try the Aztec Warrior elixir, a blend of chocolate and spices inspired by ancient Aztec recipes.

El Farol's Secret Courtyard - 808 Canyon Rd, Santa Fe, NM 87501

El Farol, Santa Fe's oldest restaurant and bar, has a secret back courtyard perfect for intimate gatherings. It's a beautiful spot for enjoying their famous tapas and cocktails.

How to Access: Ask a server to direct you to the courtyard when you arrive.

La Reina at El Rey Court - 1862 Cerrillos Rd, Santa Fe, NM 87505

La Reina is a stylish tequila and mezcal bar that feels like a speakeasy hidden within the eclectic El Rey Court. Known for its unique ambiance, it's where locals go for well-crafted cocktails.

Insider Tip: Don't miss their weekly live music nights featuring local musicians.

Piedra Lisa Trail – Petroglyph Site - Located just outside of Santa Fe

This trail is off the beaten path and features petroglyphs carved by ancient Puebloans. The rugged terrain offers a sense of solitude and an incredible look into history.

> *Insider Tip: The trail is not marked, so bring a map or GPS. It's a rewarding find for those interested in ancient art and history.*

CHAPTER 11

OUTDOOR ACTIVITIES – EMBRACING SANTA FE'S NATURAL SPLENDOR

With its high desert location and the majestic Sangre de Cristo Mountains in its backyard, Santa Fe is a haven for nature lovers, adventure seekers, and those yearning for a break in breathtaking landscapes. From tranquil hiking trails to heart-pounding adventures, Santa Fe offers a range of outdoor experiences that are truly unique.

HIKING TRAILS AND NATURE WALKS

Dale Ball Trails - Near Upper Canyon Rd, Santa Fe, NM 87501

Located just a stone's throw away from downtown, the Dale Ball Trails present a network of interconnected paths that are clearly marked and cater to all levels of hikers. Meandering through piñon and juniper-covered hills, these trails offer sweeping vistas of Santa Fe and the surrounding mountains, making them a convenient and picturesque choice for outdoor enthusiasts.

> *Insider Tip: The trail system has several access points, but parking near the Sierra del Norte trailhead offers direct access to some of the most scenic sections.*

Atalaya Mountain Trail - Trailhead at St. John's College, Santa Fe, NM 87505

This moderate to challenging trail leads hikers through fragrant ponderosa pine forests, culminating in stunning 360-degree views of the city and the surrounding mountains. The Atalaya Mountain Trail is about 6 miles round-trip and is perfect for those craving a rewarding climb.

The Atalaya Mountain Trail has become a cherished tradition in our family. Greg and I, along with our kids and grandkids, have hiked it numerous times, making sure to take plenty of breaks for water and snacks. The view of the sunset from the summit is a memory we all treasure, making this trail a perfect choice for families looking for a memorable outdoor adventure.

Santa Fe Canyon Preserve - 1160 Upper Canyon Rd, Santa Fe, NM 87501

This lesser-known preserve is home to easy walking trails through peaceful meadows and along a flowing stream. It's a serene spot for birdwatching, and visitors can enjoy a historic glimpse of Santa Fe's water reservoirs.

> *Insider Tip: Early morning is the best time to visit, as you'll likely spot various bird species, including hummingbirds and red-tailed hawks.*

Bandelier National Monument - 15 Entrance Rd, Los Alamos, NM 87544

A short drive from Santa Fe, Bandelier offers a fascinating blend of nature and history. The Main Loop Trail leads you to ancient cliff dwellings, petroglyphs, and scenic views of Frijoles Canyon. For a more adventurous hike, the Alcove House Trail includes ladders that take you to cliffside ruins.

> **Fun Fact:** *The monument has a unique "Leave No Trace" program that encourages visitors to pack out everything they bring in to preserve its beauty.*

Sun Mountain Trail - Access from Sun Mountain Trailhead, Camino de Cruz Blanca, Santa Fe, NM 87505

This shorter hike leads to panoramic views of the Santa Fe landscape. While it's less crowded than other trails, it's equally breathtaking and suitable for a quick adventure.

> **Insider Tip:** *Visit at sunrise or sunset for the most spectacular views, and you'll have the mountain almost to yourself.*

Kasha-Katuwe Tent Rocks National Monument - 40 miles southwest of Santa Fe, off NM-22

Known for its cone-shaped rock formations, Tent Rocks offers trails that weave through these unique geological structures. The Slot Canyon Trail is especially popular and provides an exciting walk through narrow rock passageways.

> **Insider Tip:** *Tent Rocks can get hot during the day, so bring plenty of water and try to arrive early, especially during the summer.*

Aspen Vista Trail - Hyde Park Rd, near Ski Santa Fe

This trail is renowned for its spectacular aspen groves that turn vibrant gold in the fall, creating a scene straight out of a painting. It's a favorite among photographers and families, with easy sections perfect for all ages.

Fun Fact: The trail offers some of the best autumn foliage in New Mexico, and during peak season, it becomes a popular spot for locals and visitors alike.

ADRENALINE-PUMPING ADVENTURES

White Water Rafting on the Rio Grande

The Rio Grande offers various white water rafting experiences, from calmer sections for beginners to thrilling Class III and IV rapids in the Taos Box. You'll wind through dramatic canyons with breathtaking views at every turn.

How to Book: With local outfitters like Kokopelli Rafting Adventures or New Mexico River Adventures

Our first time rafting here was unforgettable. The guide made it fun and safe, and the thrill of the rapids was exhilarating. It's a must-do for anyone who loves the water and a bit of adventure.

Ski Santa Fe - 1477 NM-475, Santa Fe, NM 87501

Just 16 miles from downtown, Ski Santa Fe offers skiing and snowboarding trails for all skill levels. In addition to skiing, there's a cozy lodge where visitors can enjoy a warm drink while taking in stunning alpine views.

> *Insider Tip: If you're new to skiing, Ski Santa Fe offers group lessons and rentals, making it easy to get started. For a beautiful off-season experience, visit the area in autumn to ride the chairlift and enjoy the fall foliage.*

Mountain Biking on La Tierra Trails - 599 Bypass, Santa Fe, NM 87506

La Tierra Trails offer a variety of trails for mountain bikers, from beginner-friendly paths to challenging, rugged terrain. The trails wind through high desert landscapes, providing scenic views and a thrilling ride.

> *Fun Fact: La Tierra Trails are often used for mountain biking competitions and host a vibrant community of local riders.*

Rock Climbing at Diablo Canyon - Located northwest of Santa Fe

This scenic canyon is a haven for rock climbers, featuring basalt cliffs with routes for all levels. Diablo Canyon is popular with locals and a fantastic place to try climbing in an awe-inspiring setting.

> *Insider Tip:* If you're new to rock climbing, consider booking a guided climb with a local outfitter to explore this unique area safely.

Zip Lining at Ski Santa Fe - 1477 NM-475, Santa Fe, NM 87501

During the summer months, Ski Santa Fe offers an exhilarating zip-lining experience that provides stunning mountain views from high above the forest floor. Rest assured, it's a safe and thrilling way to take in the beautiful landscape.

> *Insider Tip:* Book your zip-line tour in advance, as it's a popular attraction and fills up quickly, especially on weekends.

Balloon Rides over Santa Fe

A hot air balloon ride over the high desert is an unforgettable experience. Float over stunning landscapes, taking in panoramic views of Santa Fe and beyond. Sunrise flights offer the most vivid colors and the calmest air.

How to Book: With companies like **Santa Fe Balloons**

Taking a sunrise balloon ride over Santa Fe is breathtaking. Watching the sunrise over the desert landscape was a serene yet exhilarating experience I'll never forget.

SCENIC DRIVES AND DAY TRIPS

High Road to Taos

This scenic byway winds through mountain villages, historic churches, and rolling hills, showcasing New Mexico's cultural richness. Along the way, visit the town of Chimayo and its famous church, or stop for art galleries in Truchas.

> *Insider Tip: Don't miss a visit to **El Santuario de Chimayo**, known for its holy dirt, which many believe has healing properties.*

Abiquiú and Ghost Ranch

Head northwest of Santa Fe to explore the landscapes that inspired Georgia O'Keeffe's paintings. Ghost Ranch offers hiking trails and museums that explore O'Keeffe's legacy, while nearby Abiquiú is a charming village with stunning views.

> *Fun Fact: Ghost Ranch also offers horseback riding through its stunning red rock landscapes.*

Turquoise Trail

This historic route between Santa Fe and Albuquerque winds through the Ortiz Mountains and the colorful town of Madrid, once a booming coal mining town. Today, it's known for quirky art galleries, cafes, and gift shops.

> *Fun Fact: Stop at **Maggie's Diner** in Madrid, a filming location for the movie* Wild Hogs. *It's an actual gift shop now, selling memorabilia and unique items.*

Jemez Mountains Scenic Byway

This drive takes you through lush mountain landscapes, red rock cliffs, and natural hot springs. The Jemez Mountains are a perfect day trip with numerous hiking trails, picnic areas, and scenic overlooks.

> *Fun Fact: On the drive, you'll pass the* Valles Caldera, *a massive volcanic crater that's a National Preserve with incredible wildlife viewing opportunities.*

Pecos National Historical **Park**

Just 25 miles from Santa Fe, this park combines natural beauty with historical significance. Visitors can explore ancient ruins, historic battle sites, and walking trails that offer beautiful views of the Pecos River.

> *Insider Tip:* The park occasionally hosts star-gazing events, making it an amazing nighttime destination.

White Rock Overlook - Overlook Rd, White Rock, NM 87544

About a 30-minute drive from Santa Fe, this overlook provides jaw-dropping views of the Rio Grande Valley. It's a peaceful spot to watch the sunset and take in the surrounding mesas.

Greg and I often bring a picnic dinner to White Rock Overlook—it's a tranquil spot, and the views are unbeatable.

Experience Santa Fe's stunning natural beauty through serene hikes, thrilling adventures, and unforgettable scenic drives. Whether you're a dedicated outdoor enthusiast or someone looking to explore at a leisurely pace, Santa Fe offers outdoor activities that showcase the city's diverse and awe-inspiring landscapes.

CHAPTER 12

INDOOR ACTIVITIES – DISCOVERING SANTA FE'S ARTISTIC SOUL AND COZY HIDEAWAYS

When it comes to indoor experiences, Santa Fe offers a rich array of cultural attractions, creative spaces, and tranquil retreats. Whether you're interested in art, literature, or a cozy place to sip coffee on a chilly day, this chapter highlights some of the best indoor activities to experience the City Different.

MUSEUMS AND ART GALLERIES

Georgia O'Keeffe Museum - 217 Johnson St, Santa Fe, NM 87501

Dedicated to the life and work of Georgia O'Keeffe, this museum houses a vast collection of her paintings, sketches, and personal items. As you wander through the galleries, you'll gain insight into O'Keeffe's artistic journey and her deep connection to the New Mexican landscape.

Every visit to the Georgia O'Keeffe Museum is a journey into the vibrant colors and spirit of Santa Fe, as captured in O'Keeffe's paintings. Greg and I have spent many afternoons here, lost in her works, and each visit feels like a new perspective on Santa Fe through her eyes.

Museum of International Folk Art - 706 Camino Lejo, Santa Fe, NM 87505

Home to an impressive collection of folk art from around the globe, this museum celebrates the vibrant crafts, textiles, and cultural expressions of artists worldwide. The Girard Wing, in particular, is a visual feast with over 100,000 pieces displayed in vibrant dioramas.

> *Insider Tip: Don't miss the interactive exhibits at the Museum of International Folk Art. They provide a unique and engaging way to experience folk art, making it a great spot for children or anyone who enjoys a hands-on approach to culture.*
>
> *Fun Fact: This museum holds the largest collection of international folk art in the world.*

SITE Santa Fe - 1606 Paseo de Peralta, Santa Fe, NM 87501

SITE Santa Fe is a contemporary art space showcasing cutting-edge, thought-provoking works by local and international artists. Exhibitions here often focus on socially relevant themes, making it a must-visit for anyone interested in modern art.

Insider Tip: Check their calendar for artist talks and panel
discussions, which provide an insider perspective on the
exhibits.

*I remember attending a multi-sensory exhibit here with
Channa. We spent hours exploring, marveling at the way
art can express the complexities of the human experience.*

New Mexico Museum of Art - 107 W Palace Ave, Santa Fe, NM
87501

Housed in a stunning Pueblo Revival-style building, the New Mexico
Museum of Art features an impressive collection of Southwestern art.
Its permanent collection spans various eras, offering insights into the
region's cultural evolution.

Fun Fact: This museum is the oldest art museum in the state,
having opened in 1917. Its courtyard is also one of the
most picturesque spots in Santa Fe.

Museum of Indian Arts & Culture - 710 Camino Lejo, Santa Fe, NM
87505

This museum showcases the art, culture, and heritage of the Native
peoples of the Southwest. Its exhibits include pottery, jewelry, and
textiles, as well as cultural artifacts that provide a window into
indigenous history.

Insider Tip: The museum's "Here, Now and Always" exhibit
is particularly captivating, featuring interactive elements
that enhance the storytelling experience.

COZY CAFES AND BOOKSTORES

Iconik Coffee Roasters - 1600 Lena St, Santa Fe, NM 87505

Known for its cozy atmosphere and specialty coffee, Iconik is a beloved local spot where you can enjoy artisan roasts, delicious pastries, and a laid-back vibe. It's the perfect place to relax, read a book, or catch up with friends.

> *Greg and I had our first date at Iconik Coffee Roasters, sharing coffee and a slice of their homemade carrot cake. This place holds a special place in my heart, and I often return to bask in its comfortable ambiance and the memories it holds.*

Collected Works Bookstore & Coffeehouse - 202 Galisteo St, Santa Fe, NM 87501

This independent bookstore has an extensive collection of regional books, fiction, and non-fiction, along with a cozy coffeehouse. Collected Works often hosts author events and book signings, making it a cultural hub for the literary community.

> *Insider Tip: Look out for their poetry readings and writing workshops. It's a great way to meet local authors and fellow book lovers.*

Op.Cit Books - DeVargas Center, 157 Paseo de Peralta, Santa Fe, NM 87501

This charming bookstore offers a curated selection of books, including rare finds and regional titles. It's a quiet, cozy spot to browse for a new read.

Fun Fact: The owner, Jared, is often there and loves chatting about books. Ask him for recommendations.

The Teahouse - 821 Canyon Rd, Santa Fe, NM 87501

Situated along Canyon Road, The Teahouse offers an extensive menu of teas from around the world, accompanied by delicious, healthy food. The cozy, tranquil ambiance is perfect for a relaxing afternoon.

Insider Tip: Try their lavender Earl Grey and the chai latte. They also have a lovely outdoor seating area for enjoying tea al fresco.

Java Joe's - 2801 Rodeo Rd, Santa Fe, NM 87505

A beloved local hangout, Java Joe's is known for its quirky decor, relaxed atmosphere, and fantastic coffee. Their breakfast burritos and homemade pastries are popular with locals.

Fun Fact: Java Joe's often features live music, so you can enjoy your coffee with some tunes.

PERFORMING ARTS VENUES

The Lensic Performing Arts Center - 211 W San Francisco St, Santa Fe, NM 87501

Originally built in 1931, The Lensic hosts various events, from concerts and theater productions to film screenings and lectures. The beautifully restored theater is an iconic venue that's central to Santa Fe's performing arts scene.

Insider Tip: Check their calendar for free community events, like live jazz performances and cultural lectures.

SANTA FE OPERA HOUSE - 301 Opera Dr, Santa Fe, NM 87506

Renowned for its open-air design, the Santa Fe Opera offers world-class productions with a stunning mountain backdrop. Even if you're not an opera enthusiast, the experience of watching a performance here is magical.

> *Greg and I recently saw our first concert at the opera house and have decided to make it a summer tradition to attend at least one event there. There's something magical about watching the sunset behind the stage as the show begins.*

Santa Fe Playhouse - 142 E De Vargas St, Santa Fe, NM 87501

Founded in 1919, the Santa Fe Playhouse is one of the oldest community theaters in the country. The playhouse showcases a mix of classic and contemporary plays, fostering local talent and creativity.

> **Fun Fact:** *Their annual "Fiesta Melodrama" is a local favorite, featuring satirical sketches about Santa Fe and its colorful history.*

Teatro Paraguas - 3205 Calle Marie, Santa Fe, NM 87507

Teatro Paraguas is a small theater dedicated to bilingual and multicultural performances. Their programming often highlights Hispanic and Native American voices, offering a unique perspective on Santa Fe's cultural landscape.

> **Insider Tip:** *They frequently hold poetry readings and community events, which are a great way to experience local talent in an intimate setting.*

Armory for the Arts Theater - 1050 Old Pecos Trail, Santa Fe, NM 87505

This versatile venue hosts a variety of performances, including theater productions, concerts, and dance performances. It's a community-focused space that provides a platform for emerging artists.

> *Insider Tip:* Keep an eye out for local theater company performances, which showcase the depth of Santa Fe's creative talent.

Santa Fe's indoor activities offer a range of cultural and cozy experiences, from exploring world-renowned art collections to relaxing with a book in a quaint café. Whether you're looking for artistic inspiration, a quiet corner to read, or an evening of theater, the City Different offers a diverse range of indoor activities to suit every interest.

CHAPTER 13

ACTIVITIES FOR ALL SEASONS – EMBRACING SANTA FE YEAR-ROUND

Santa Fe is a destination that captivates visitors with its diverse range of activities in every season. Whether it's skiing in the winter, exploring the blooming gardens in the spring, enjoying the vibrant festivals in summer, or admiring the breathtaking autumn foliage, there's always something exciting to do. Here's how to experience the best of Santa Fe all year round.

WINTER WONDERLAND: SKIING, LIGHTS, AND FESTIVITIES

Ski Santa Fe - 1477 NM-475, Santa Fe, NM 87501

Nestled high in the Sangre de Cristo Mountains, Ski Santa Fe offers skiers and snowboarders a range of slopes suited to every skill level. The resort provides beautiful views of snow-covered peaks and well-groomed trails, with rentals and lessons available for beginners.

Insider Tip: After a day on the slopes, head to the Totemoff's Bar at mid-mountain for a warm drink and incredible views. They also have live music on weekends, making it a great après-ski spot.

Farolito Walk on Canyon Road - Canyon Road, Santa Fe, NM 87501

A beloved Christmas Eve tradition, the Farolito Walk transforms Canyon Road into a glowing wonderland. Farolitos (small paper lanterns) line the streets and pathways, illuminating the galleries and shops that stay open late while carolers fill the air with holiday songs. This tradition, which dates back to the Spanish colonial period, symbolizes the lighting of the way for the Christ child. It's a beautiful and unique way to experience the holiday season in Santa Fe.

Insider Tip: Arrive early to find parking and dress warmly, as temperatures drop quickly. For a special treat, grab a hot chocolate from a local café to enjoy during the walk.

SANTA FE WINTER **Indian Market** - La Fonda on the Plaza, 100 E San Francisco St, Santa Fe, NM 87501

Held each December, this indoor market brings together Native American artists from across the country. Browse exquisite handcrafted jewelry, pottery, and textiles while learning about the rich cultural heritage of the artists.

> *Fun Fact: This is one of the few opportunities to see some of the same artists featured in the Summer Indian Market but in a more intimate, indoor setting.*

Ojo Caliente Mineral Springs Resort & Spa - 50 Los Banos Dr, Ojo Caliente, NM 87549

A short drive from Santa Fe, Ojo Caliente offers hot mineral springs perfect for soaking in the winter. The pools are rich in various minerals believed to have therapeutic properties, and the tranquil setting in the snowy desert landscape is breathtaking.

> *Insider Tip: Visit in the evening when the pools are illuminated under the stars, creating a magical experience. Be sure to book your visit in advance during peak seasons. To book your visit, you can either call the resort directly or use their online booking system. Keep in mind that weekends and holidays tend to fill up quickly, so it's best to book as early as possible.*

Annual Posadas Procession - Santa Fe Plaza, Downtown Santa Fe

Held in December, this traditional re-enactment of Mary and Joseph's search for lodging is a cherished local event. The procession moves through the Plaza, with participants carrying candles, singing carols, and celebrating with hot cider and biscochitos (traditional New Mexican cookies).

Greg and I enjoy this yearly tradition. It's such a warm, community-focused way to get into the holiday spirit, and the biscochitos are a delicious treat.

SPRING BLOOMS: GARDENS, FESTIVALS, AND NEW BEGINNINGS

Santa Fe Botanical Garden - 715 Camino Lejo, Santa Fe, NM 87505

As winter gives way to spring, the Botanical Garden comes alive with vibrant blooms and lush landscapes. Themed sections like the Ojos y Manos Garden showcase native plants, while the Orchard Gardens feature blossoming fruit trees.

> *Insider Tip: Visit in April when the garden hosts spring-themed events, including plant sales and guided tours focusing on seasonal plants.*

Santa Fe Renaissance Fair - El Rancho de las Golondrinas, 334 Los Pinos Rd, Santa Fe, NM 87507

Step back in time at this lively fair featuring jousting tournaments, costumed performers, and artisanal crafts. Held in the spring, the Renaissance Fair is a family-friendly event where you can enjoy turkey legs, live music, and traditional games.

> *Fun Fact: El Rancho de las Golondrinas is a historic site that regularly hosts living history events, adding an authentic touch to the fair.*

MEOW WOLF'S Annual Float Parade - Rufina Street, near the Meow Wolf Art Complex

A whimsical parade of imaginative floats and costumed performers, this event is pure Meow Wolf—an unexpected and fantastical twist on the classic parade. It's a fantastic way to experience the community's creativity and the unique spirit of Santa Fe.

> *Insider Tip: Get there early to secure a spot along the parade route, and bring a camera—the floats are a sight to behold!*

Eldorado Studio Tour - Eldorado, just outside of Santa Fe

This annual event opens the doors of local artists' studios in the Eldorado neighborhood, giving visitors a chance to see where artists work and to purchase art directly from the source. It's one of Santa Fe's hidden gems, showcasing a wide range of media, from painting to sculpture to jewelry.

> *Fun Fact: The tour usually takes place over a weekend, so you can make a day of it and visit multiple studios. It's a fantastic way to discover local talent and bring home a piece of Santa Fe's art scene.*

SUMMER ESCAPES: CONCERTS, ART, AND OUTDOOR FUN

Santa Fe Bandstand - Santa Fe Plaza, Downtown Santa Fe

Running from June to August, the Santa Fe Bandstand series offers free outdoor concerts featuring diverse musical genres. Locals and visitors gather in the Plaza, relaxing on blankets and enjoying warm summer nights filled with music.

> *Insider Tip: Bring a picnic or grab some food from one of the nearby vendors or restaurants. It's a perfect way to enjoy Santa Fe's summer evenings.*

Santa Fe Opera Tailgate Parties - 301 Opera Dr, Santa Fe, NM 87506

Tailgating at the Santa Fe Opera is more than just a pre-show ritual; it's an iconic tradition that fosters a sense of community. Before performances, patrons set up picnics in the parking lot, often with elaborate spreads. It's a social event that brings together opera-goers of all ages for food, drinks, and conversation before the show.

> *Insider Tip: Arrive early for the best spots, and bring a table and chairs. Some people go all-out with their tailgate setups, and it's fun to walk around and see the creativity on display.*

Santa Fe Indian Market - Santa Fe Plaza, Downtown Santa Fe

Held in August, this market is one of the largest and most prestigious Native American art markets in the world. Over 1,000 artists from various tribes gather to showcase and sell their work, including jewelry, pottery, and textiles.

> *Fun Fact: Many of the artists come from families who have participated in the market for generations. It's an incredible opportunity to purchase authentic Native American art and meet the artists behind the pieces.*

Pecos River Tubing - Pecos River, near Pecos, NM

For a fun and refreshing summer activity, there's nothing quite like tubing down the Pecos River. The gentle currents make it a relaxing way to enjoy the warm weather and stunning mountain views, providing a perfect escape from the hustle and bustle of daily life.

> *Insider Tip:* Rent tubes from a local outfitter, and pack a waterproof bag for snacks and sunscreen. It's a great way to spend a day with friends or family.

FALL FOLIAGE: HARVEST CELEBRATIONS, ART WALKS, AND SCENIC DRIVES

Santa Fe Wine Harvest Festival - Various wineries and the Santa Fe Opera

The Santa Fe Wine Harvest Festival is a unique celebration that takes place at various wineries and the Santa Fe Opera. It's a wonderful opportunity to taste the region's finest wines, enjoy live music, and learn about the winemaking process. Celebrate the grape harvest with wine tastings, live music, and food pairings. Held in late September, this festival brings together local wineries and chefs, offering a delightful way to savor the flavors of Santa Fe.

> *Insider Tip:* Purchase tickets early, as the event often sells out. It's a popular festival with locals and visitors alike.

Scenic Drive to the Sangre de Cristo Mountains - Start on Hyde Park Road, leading up to Ski Santa Fe

The Sangre de Cristo Mountains burst into color in the fall, with aspen trees turning golden. Take a scenic drive or hike the Aspen Vista Trail for breathtaking foliage views.

Greg and I take this drive every fall—it's our yearly tradition. We pack a picnic, bring a camera, and make a day of exploring the mountains. The fall colors are truly spectacular.

Zozobra Burning - Fort Marcy Park, Santa Fe, NM

Part of the annual Fiesta de Santa Fe, the Zozobra burning is a unique event where a giant marionette effigy is set ablaze, symbolizing the burning away of gloom. It's a one-of-a-kind tradition that draws crowds from all over.

> *Insider Tip:* Arrive early to get a good viewing spot, and prepare for fireworks and a lively crowd. It's an unforgettable way to experience Santa Fe's quirky side.

Abiquiú Studio Tour - Abiquiú, NM

Each October, the Abiquiú Studio Tour invites visitors into the studios of local artists, including some in the same landscapes that inspired Georgia O'Keeffe. It's a chance to see incredible art and explore the stunning autumn landscapes of Northern New Mexico.

Fun Fact: Abiquiú is known for its striking rock formations and desert vistas. The fall colors combined with the art make this a must-see event for art lovers and nature enthusiasts.

Each season in Santa Fe offers something new and enchanting. From the snowy mountains of winter to the blooming gardens of spring, the lively festivals of summer, and the golden hues of autumn, the City Different is a year-round destination for those who seek adventure, culture, and the beauty of nature.

CHAPTER 14
TOP 10 HIDDEN GEMS AND TOURIST TRAPS IN SANTA FE

TOP 10 HIDDEN GEMS

Railyard Artisan Market - 1607 Paseo de Peralta, Santa Fe, NM 87501

This exclusive Sunday market, the Railyard Artisan Market, is a showcase of a rotating selection of handmade crafts, fresh produce, and art from local artisans. You'll find unique treasures here that capture the essence of Santa Fe's creative spirit, making you feel like a privileged guest in the city, enjoying an experience that few others have the opportunity to.

> *Insider Tip: Be proactive and arrive early to secure the best picks, as popular items like handcrafted pottery and locally grown produce, typically ranging from $ 10 to $ 100, sell out quickly. Enjoy a fresh pastry as you browse, feeling ahead of the game.*

WHEELWRIGHT MUSEUM of the American Indian - 704 Camino Lejo, Santa Fe, NM 87505

Focused on Native American art and culture, the Wheelwright Museum is a serene oasis, offering a peaceful respite from the city's hustle and bustle. It's an excellent spot for exploring traditional and contemporary Native American art, allowing you to relax and immerse yourself in the culture, feeling at peace in the midst of the city's hustle and bustle.

> *Fun Fact: The museum's Case Trading Post is one of the best places in town to buy authentic Native American jewelry and pottery, with pieces created by both emerging and established artists.*

Ghost Ranch Education & Retreat Center - 280 Private Dr 1708, Abiquiú, NM 87510

This stunning retreat was one of artist Georgia O'Keeffe's favorite places for inspiration. Visitors can hike, take art workshops, or explore the incredible landscapes that inspired much of her work.

> *Insider Tip: Sign up for a fossil tour and discover ancient remnants of when New Mexico was an ocean! Perfect for anyone curious about the area's prehistoric past.*

El Farol's Flamenco Nights - 808 Canyon Rd, Santa Fe, NM 87501

This historic bar, El Farol, offers lively flamenco performances, delicious tapas, and a rich history dating back to 1835. The intimate setting and authentic performances make it the perfect place to experience passionate dance and music, enriching your cultural experience in Santa Fe and making you feel truly immersed in the local culture, not just a spectator but a part of the vibrant scene.

> *Fun Fact: It's Santa Fe's oldest restaurant, and rumor has it that a few ghosts enjoy the shows as much as the patrons do. If you're intrigued by the paranormal, ask the staff about its haunted history.*

The Jean Cocteau Cinema - 418 Montezuma Ave, Santa Fe, NM 87501

Owned by George R.R. Martin, this quirky cinema is a great spot to catch indie films, cult classics, and author events. Perfect for film buffs and fans of Martin's work!

> *Insider Tip: Watch their event schedule—you might be able to catch a special appearance by local authors or filmmakers.*

The Monk's Corner Taproom - 205 W San Francisco St, Santa Fe, NM 87501

Tucked away from the main tourist crowds, this rustic taproom serves local craft beers in a relaxed setting. The staff is knowledgeable and friendly, making it a favorite hangout for locals.

> *Fun Fact: The building is over a century old, and stepping inside feels like stepping back in time. Ask the staff for beer recommendations—they love to share their favorites.*

La Choza Patio - 905 Alarid St, Santa Fe, NM 87505

La Choza is a go-to spot for locals craving authentic New Mexican food, but the patio dining experience is where the real magic happens. Relax with a margarita and carne adovada as the sun sets.

> *Insider Tip: Try the sopapillas with honey for dessert—a local favorite. They're the perfect ending to a hearty meal.*

El Museo Cultural de Santa Fe - 555 Camino de la Familia, Santa Fe, NM 87501

This museum offers exhibits, swap meets, and live music that celebrates Hispanic and Latino culture in Santa Fe. It's a fantastic spot for a deep dive into the local heritage.

> *Fun Fact: Their events include everything from salsa dancing to art shows, so check their calendar for unique local happenings.*

Baca Street Arts District - 926 Baca St, Santa Fe, NM 87505

This artsy neighborhood is home to quirky galleries, studios, and shops. It's a hidden gem for those looking to discover Santa Fe's lesser-known artists.

> *Insider Tip: Stop by Liquid Light Glass to watch glassblowing demonstrations or take a class yourself. It's a memorable experience you can take home with you.*

Skylight Rooftop Concerts - 139 W San Francisco St, Santa Fe, NM 87501

Enjoy live music on the rooftop while soaking in views of Santa Fe and the mountains. It's a secret spot for music lovers seeking a chill, intimate venue.

> *Insider Tip: Arrive at sunset for beautiful views paired with*

great music. Check their social media for the latest event announcements.

TOP 10 TOURIST TRAPS TO AVOID

Overpriced Guided Nature Tours

These tours charge high prices for basic hikes in popular areas, often covering trails that are free and easy to explore on your own.

> *Better Alternative: Use local trail maps or apps to hike independently. Trails like the Dale Ball Trails are well-marked and easy to navigate solo.*

Horse-Drawn Carriage Rides

While picturesque, these rides can be pricey and cover a limited route.

> *Better Alternative: Take a walking tour for a more flexible way to experience the city's sights up close and at your own pace.*

Mass-Market Southwestern Jewelry Shops

Many shops near the Plaza sell mass-produced jewelry marketed as "authentic." Prices are often high, and the items lack true artisanal craftsmanship.

> *Better Alternative: Shop at reputable stores or directly from artisans who can certify their work as authentic. For genuine, handmade Native American jewelry, try:*
> ~ ***Cutting Edge Turquoise*** *– cuttingedgeturquoise.com*
> ~ ***Sunwest on the Plaza*** *– 66 E San Francisco St*

Santa Fe Trolley Tours

These tours tend to be crowded and pricey and offer limited flexibility.

> *Better Alternative: Look for smaller group or private tours that provide a more personalized experience.*

Plaza Street Performers

Some performers can be entertaining, but others may pressure tourists for tips.

> *Better Alternative: Check out live music at local venues for a more authentic experience with talented local musicians.*

Mass-Produced Crafts at Indian Market

Some vendors at the Indian Market sell mass-produced items.

> *Better Alternative: Seek booths with handmade pieces and chat with the artists to ensure you're supporting authentic Native American crafts.*

Overpriced Art on Canyon Road

Some galleries on Canyon Road have tourist markups on artwork.

> *Better Alternative: Explore areas like the Baca Street Arts District for better deals and unique works by lesser-known artists.*

Santa Fe Ghost Tours

While these tours are fun, they often feature exaggerated stories and high prices.

> *Better Alternative: Explore the city's haunted history with a self-guided tour or a guide known for genuine storytelling.*

High-Priced Plaza Restaurants

Plaza area restaurants tend to have higher prices due to heavy tourist traffic.

> *Better Alternative: Venture a bit further from the Plaza for equally delicious yet more affordable dining options.*

"Private" Art Show Scams

In recent years, a few pop-up "galleries" around the Plaza area have advertised "exclusive" or "private" art shows featuring supposedly original Native American art or Southwestern crafts. These events often involve high-pressure sales tactics, and unfortunately, the pieces sold are sometimes mass-produced replicas rather than authentic, locally crafted art.

__Better Alternative:__ For genuine Southwestern art, explore established galleries like the Wheelwright Museum's Case Trading Post or check out the annual Indian Market, where you can meet the artists and ensure you're supporting authentic Native American craftsmanship. You'll find unique, high-quality pieces that truly represent the local culture, often with a story to go along with them!

With these insights, visitors can confidently explore Santa Fe's vibrant culture, art, and local experiences, steering clear of common tourist traps and discovering the true heart of the City Different!

CHAPTER 15

CELEBRATING CULTURE YEAR-ROUND: SANTA FE'S TOP EVENTS AND FESTIVALS

Santa Fe's annual events and festivals, scattered across the city, are an essential part of its charm, celebrating the rich heritage, arts, and culture of the "City Different." From renowned art markets to lively music festivals, each season offers unique experiences. Here's a guide to Santa Fe's must-attend events, complete with insider tips to help you enjoy them like a local.

WinterBrew (January)

Immerse yourself in the unique experiences of WinterBrew, where local brewers showcase their creations amidst live music and a variety of food options. This cozy indoor escape in January is not just a beer festival, but a celebration of local creativity and community.

> *Insider Tip: Tickets often sell out, so purchase them in advance. Bring a notebook to jot down your favorites, as some brews are only available at the festival.*

Santa Fe Restaurant Week (February)

Start the year with a culinary journey that won't break the bank during Santa Fe Restaurant Week. Top restaurants around the city offer special prix-fixe menus, giving diners a chance to sample their creations at an affordable price. It's a perfect opportunity to indulge in high-end dining without the high-end price tag.

> *Insider Tip: Make reservations early, especially at popular spots like Geronimo and Sazón. This event is a perfect time to try multiple restaurants—consider planning for a few different dining experiences throughout the week.*

Santa Fe Film Festival (February/March)

This festival celebrates independent filmmaking, drawing film lovers to screenings, panel discussions, and special events. It's an opportunity to see films from around the world and engage with filmmakers.

> *Insider Tip: Watch for screenings at Jean Cocteau Cinema, owned by George R.R. Martin, who often hosts special Q&A sessions. Check the schedule for any unique events tied to the festival.*
> *Fun Fact: Santa Fe has a deep connection to the film industry. Don't be surprised to see some familiar faces—actors and filmmakers are frequent visitors.*

Rodeo de Santa Fe (June)

Experience the Wild West at the Rodeo de Santa Fe, which features bull riding, barrel racing, and more. The rodeo has been a Santa Fe tradition since 1949 and attracts some of the best rodeo athletes in the country.

Insider Tip: It's a family-friendly event, with activities like mutton busting for the kids. Wear a hat and sunscreen, as most events are during the day.

Santa Fe International Folk Art Market (July)

This iconic event is not just a market but a global celebration of art and culture. The Santa Fe International Folk Art Market brings artists from over 50 countries to Santa Fe, showcasing a vibrant array of textiles, ceramics, jewelry, and more, all created using traditional methods. It's a unique opportunity to experience the world's diverse artistic heritage in one place.

Insider Tip: Get there early on the first day for the best selection, and don't miss the "Global Village" area for authentic international food.

Fun Fact: Almost 90% of the proceeds go directly back to the artists and their communities, so your purchases help support cultural preservation.

Traditional Spanish Market (July)

On the Plaza, this market celebrates Spanish Colonial art forms, from tinwork to textiles. Artists demonstrate traditional methods, and the event features live music and dance performances.

Insider Tip: Come early on Sunday to avoid crowds, and take the opportunity to chat with artists about their work. Many pieces are available for purchase, and you'll find some truly unique creations.

Fun Fact: This market has been a Santa Fe tradition for over 70 years, with many artists tracing their craft back through generations.

Santa Fe Indian Market (August)

The largest Native American art market in the world, the Indian Market is a showcase of Native American craftsmanship, from jewelry and pottery to contemporary art. Artists from all over the country gather to present their work.

> *Insider Tip: Saturday morning is the busiest, so arrive early for the best selection. Side streets often have smaller, emerging artists with unique pieces.*

Santa Fe Bandstand (Summer)

Enjoy free outdoor concerts at Santa Fe Bandstand on the historic Plaza. The concert series features a diverse lineup, from local bands to national touring acts, and the whole community comes out to enjoy the music.

> *Insider Tip: Bring a blanket or a folding chair and arrive early to get a good spot. It's also a perfect chance to enjoy a picnic under the stars while listening to great music.*

Santa Fe Opera Tailgate Parties (Summer)

Tailgating at the Santa Fe Opera is an experience unlike any other. Before the show, patrons gather in the parking lot with gourmet picnics, wine, and views of the stunning sunset. Once the show starts, the magic continues inside the open-air theater.

> *Insider Tip: Bring folding chairs and enjoy a relaxed pre-show meal with fellow opera lovers. Binoculars are also handy for the performance!*

Santa Fe Fiesta and the Burning of Zozobra (Labor Day Weekend)

Santa Fe's oldest festival, dating back to 1712, celebrates the Spanish resettlement of the city. The Burning of Zozobra, or "Old Man Gloom," kicks off the event, symbolizing the purging of sorrows from the past year.

> *Insider Tip: For the best view of Zozobra, arrive early and bring a jacket, as it can get cool in the evening. Participate in the tradition by writing down your own "glooms" to add to the bonfire.*

Fiesta de los Niños at El Rancho de las Golondrinas (September)

This family-friendly event, held at the living history museum El Rancho de las Golondrinas, celebrates New Mexico's heritage with interactive activities, crafts, and performances for kids of all ages.

> *Insider Tip: Wear comfortable shoes, as you'll be exploring outdoor areas. Kids will love hands-on activities like bread baking and tin stamping!*
>
> *Fun Fact: The museum's historic buildings date back to the 18th century, providing an immersive look into colonial life.*

Santa Fe Wine and Chile Fiesta (September)

This popular festival pairs New Mexico wines with local chiles in a celebration of Santa Fe's culinary prowess. Events include wine seminars, tastings, and cooking demonstrations by renowned chefs.

> *Insider Tip: Secure tickets for the Grand Tasting in advance, as it sells out quickly. The seminars are an excellent way to learn about pairing wine with spicy food.*

Pojoaque River Art Tour (September)

This art tour takes you through the Pojoaque Valley, where you'll find local studios and galleries showcasing paintings, sculptures, pottery, and more. It's a laid-back way to enjoy New Mexico's artistic diversity.

> *Insider Tip: This is a self-guided tour, so plan your stops ahead of time. Some studios offer live demonstrations, which give you a deeper appreciation for the artists' techniques.*

International Balloon Fiesta (October)

Just an hour away in Albuquerque, this world-renowned event fills the skies with colorful hot air balloons. The Balloon Fiesta features mass ascensions, night glows, and a festive atmosphere.

> *Insider Tip: Plan to arrive early to avoid traffic and wear layers. The early morning hours can be chilly, but temperatures rise quickly once the sun comes up.*

Farolito Walk on Canyon Road (December)

Celebrate the holidays by walking along Canyon Road, illuminated by farolitos (small paper lanterns). Art galleries stay open late, carolers fill the air with festive songs, and the streets glow with a warm, magical light.

> *Insider Tip: Bundle up—it can get chilly in December. Join in the caroling for an authentic experience!*
>
> *Fun Fact: Farolitos are made from brown paper bags, sand, and candles. This beautiful tradition lights the way and symbolizes peace and hope for the New Year.*

Santa Fe Farmers' Market (Year-Round)

Held every Saturday, the Santa Fe Farmers' Market is a local staple. Vendors offer fresh produce, handmade crafts, and delicious treats. It's a fantastic way to enjoy the flavors of New Mexico.

Insider Tip: Visit the Railyard location on Saturday
mornings for the most vendors. Try a roasted green chile
burrito for an authentic local breakfast.

Santa Fe's year-round events capture the spirit and diversity of the
city. From tasting local wines and chiles to enjoying art under the
stars, these festivals and traditions make Santa Fe a city of endless
celebration and discovery. Whether you're visiting for a weekend or a
season, there's always something happening in the City Different.

CHAPTER 16

INSIDER SECRETS FOR ATTENDING SANTA FE'S TOP EVENTS

Immerse yourself in Santa Fe's unique blend of art, music, culture, and community at its vibrant festivals and events. To fully appreciate these experiences, here are some insider tips that will help you delve deeper into the local culture and enjoy the festivities like a true Santa Fean.

Plan Ahead for the Best Experience

Many of Santa Fe's events are incredibly popular and draw large crowds. The anticipation and excitement of planning for well-attended events like the Indian Market or the Wine and Chile Fiesta can add a thrilling edge to your experience, making you eagerly look forward to the event.

> *Insider Tips: Purchase tickets as soon as they're available, as they often sell out quickly. If the event involves dining, make restaurant reservations well in advance, especially at high-demand spots like Café Pasqual's or La Plazuela.*

For major events, consider booking accommodations early, too, as hotels tend to fill up fast during peak times. For some events, you may even want to secure lodging six months to a year in advance!

Explore Beyond the Main Events

Santa Fe has a host of smaller, lesser-known events happening year-round that are waiting to be discovered. Art gallery openings, intimate live music shows, and poetry readings can offer unique glimpses into local culture, adding a sense of adventure and curiosity to your visit.

> *Insider Tips: Check out the Santa Fe Reporter or Santa Fe New Mexican for local event listings. Some of the smaller venues, like Jean Cocteau Cinema or Teatro Paraguas, often host niche performances and screenings that locals love.*

> *Take a look at community boards in coffee shops like Iconik Coffee Roasters or Downtown Subscription. You might stumble upon a local craft fair, art workshop, or live music performance that isn't advertised widely.*

Dress Smart for Santa Fe's Unique Climate

Santa Fe's high-desert climate means you can experience a wide range of temperatures in a single day. Mornings and evenings can be chilly even in summer, while daytime temps may soar.

> *Insider Tips: Dressing in layers is key! Always carry a light jacket or shawl, wear a sun hat, and apply sunscreen generously. You'll thank yourself later when temperatures fluctuate unexpectedly.*

During summer events, a refillable water bottle is essential for
staying hydrated. In winter, bring gloves, a warm hat, and
extra layers, especially if you're attending outdoor events
like the Farolito Walk on Canyon Road.

Support Local Artists and Artisans

Santa Fe's festivals and events are often focused on showcasing local talent, from Native American jewelers at the Indian Market to painters and sculptors at the Folk Art Market. Supporting local artists not only contributes to the community's creative economy but also fosters a sense of respect and appreciation for their work.

Insider Tips: Ask artists about their work, especially if you're
attending an art market or festival. Artists appreciate the
chance to share the stories behind their creations, and
you'll gain a deeper appreciation for the unique pieces
you're purchasing.

Carry cash for smaller events, as not all vendors accept cards.
It's also helpful for tipping street performers, who add a
vibrant layer to events around the Plaza or on Canyon
Road.

Use Public Transportation or Carpool When Possible

Parking can be challenging in areas like the Plaza and Railyard during big events. Public transportation or rideshare services can ease the hassle and let you enjoy the day without worrying about finding a parking spot.

Insider Tips: The Santa Fe Trails bus system has routes that
serve major event locations, and for some events, there are
shuttle services. Uber and Lyft are also available in
Santa Fe.

> *Consider carpooling with friends or fellow travelers, especially*
> *if you're staying nearby. For some larger events, parking*
> *lots fill up quickly, so plan to arrive early or take*
> *advantage of park-and-ride services.*

Embrace Santa Fe's Cultural Etiquette

Santa Fe has a deep respect for its diverse cultural heritage, which is reflected in many of its events. If you're attending events with religious or cultural significance, take time to learn about the traditions and follow any guidelines or customs.

> *Insider Tips: At Pueblo Feast Days or ceremonies, it's*
> *customary to ask permission before taking photos. Always*
> *follow any signs or requests to avoid recording or*
> *photographing specific parts of the event.*

> *Dressing modestly and being mindful of local customs is*
> *appreciated. Events such as the Burning of Zozobra or the*
> *Indian Market may have specific cultural protocols, so*
> *observing and respecting them adds to a positive*
> *experience.*

Get to Know the Locals and Engage with Community Volunteers

Many festivals and events in Santa Fe are volunteer-driven. Engaging with locals and volunteers at events is a fantastic way to hear about the history and traditions associated with them.

> *Insider Tips: Strike up conversations with volunteers—they're*
> *often happy to share insights and tips for enjoying the*
> *event. Some may even recommend additional local*
> *happenings or places to visit nearby.*

Consider volunteering for an event if you're a frequent visitor to Santa Fe. It's a rewarding way to meet locals and get an insider perspective on some of the city's most celebrated festivals.

Savor the Local Cuisine at Food Stalls and Pop-Ups

Many events feature food vendors offering authentic New Mexican cuisine. This is a great way to sample local flavors like green chile stew, blue corn tamales, and more.

Insider Tips: Don't skip the smaller, locally-owned food stalls. They often serve up some of the most authentic and delicious New Mexican dishes. Try a roasted chile-infused treat at the Santa Fe Farmers' Market or a hot cup of atole at the Winter Indian Market.

Bring cash, as some vendors only accept cash. And be adventurous! Ask vendors about their ingredients and the stories behind their dishes.

Capture the Moment—But Mindfully

Events in Santa Fe are often picturesque, making them perfect for capturing memories. But at certain culturally significant events, it's essential to be respectful when taking photos.

Insider Tips: Always ask before taking photos of people, especially at cultural or religious events. When photographing art installations or performances, be mindful of any rules or restrictions. For example, some Pueblo events have strict no-photography policies to protect their cultural heritage.

*If you're looking for a less crowded photo opportunity, visit
event venues early in the morning or just before sunset,
when the light is best and crowds may be lighter.*

Pace Yourself and Take Breaks

Many Santa Fe events are packed with activities, so it's essential to
pace yourself to enjoy the experience fully. Take time to relax, have a
bite, or simply people-watch to absorb the local ambiance.

*Insider Tips: The Plaza, Railyard Park, and other open spaces
often have shaded seating areas or grassy spots perfect for
a break. Grab a local treat—such as a blue corn atole or a
chocolate elixir from Kakawa Chocolate House—and take
a breather.*

For events with multiple venues or stages, plan your route in advance to avoid missing any must-see attractions. A little downtime can help you recharge and appreciate the full experience.

Santa Fe's festivals and events offer a vibrant mix of culture, history, and community spirit. By following these tips, you'll gain a deeper appreciation for the city's unique traditions, make the most of your experience, and even uncover some local secrets along the way. Enjoy the magic of the "City Different" and the unforgettable memories that come with it!

CHAPTER 17

PHOTOGRAPHY AND MEMORY-MAKING

Santa Fe is a photographer's dream, offering a stunning array of landscapes, architectural gems, and cultural moments. This chapter provides a guide to some of the best spots for creating unforgettable memories and capturing the essence of the "City Different."

TOP PHOTO OPPORTUNITIES AND SCENIC SPOTS

Historic Plaza

The heart of Santa Fe, the Plaza is surrounded by adobe buildings, local shops, and bustling activity. Capture the charming architecture, vibrant colors, and historic details.

> *Insider Tip: Arrive early in the morning for shots without crowds. Capture the Plaza's peacefulness as the city wakes up.*

Canyon Road

Known for its art galleries, Canyon Road is filled with colorful sculptures, stunning adobe buildings, and unique storefronts.

Insider Tip: Visit on the weekend when galleries often have artists working on-site. Engage with them to gain insights and even photograph them in action.

Cross of the Martyrs at Sunset

For one of the most breathtaking views of Santa Fe, hike up to the Cross of the Martyrs. This spot is perfect for capturing the cityscape at sunset.

Insider Tip: Bring a picnic to enjoy as you watch the sun set over the city and the mountains take on a rosy hue.

Loretto Chapel

The Loretto Chapel, famous for its "Miraculous Staircase," offers beautiful Gothic Revival architecture and intricate details.

Insider Tip: Try to visit during quieter hours to capture the staircase without crowds. The stained-glass windows also make for gorgeous close-up shots.

Bandelier National Monument

This site offers both natural beauty and cultural significance, with ancient cliff dwellings, petroglyphs, and the scenic Frijoles Canyon.

> *Insider Tip:* Visit early in the day to avoid shadows in the cliff dwellings. Pack a tripod for stable shots of the petroglyphs and the canyon.

Santa Fe Opera House

With its striking open-air design, the Opera House offers architectural beauty against the Sangre de Cristo Mountains.

> *Insider Tip:* Arrive before sunset to capture the changing colors of the sky behind the Opera House. The soft lighting complements the building's unique lines.

Santa Fe Railyard District

The Railyard is a vibrant mix of modern and historic, with its colorful murals, trendy shops, and street art. It's perfect for capturing the dynamic urban energy of Santa Fe.

> *Insider Tip:* Visit during the Farmers' Market or at dusk when the lights come on. You'll find lively street scenes and a bustling atmosphere.

Turquoise Trail National Scenic Byway

This scenic drive from Santa Fe to Albuquerque offers vast high desert landscapes, historic mining towns, and old adobe structures.

> *Insider Tip:* Stop in the artistic village of Madrid along the way for colorful buildings, quirky art installations, and unique desert views.

Santa Fe Botanical Garden

With vibrant seasonal blooms and themed gardens, this botanical garden is a sanctuary for nature photography.

> *Insider Tip: Check the garden's calendar for seasonal blooms, such as lavender in summer or fall foliage. The golden-hour lighting here is stunning.*

Sunrise at Tent Rocks

Just a short drive from Santa Fe, Kasha-Katuwe Tent Rocks National Monument offers surreal rock formations that look magical at sunrise.

> *Insider Tip: Arrive before dawn for the best light. The quiet of the early morning and the soft, golden light on the rocks make for breathtaking photos.*

TIPS FOR CAPTURING THE ESSENCE OF SANTA FE

Golden Hour Magic

Santa Fe's high desert light is at its best during the golden hour—shortly after sunrise and just before sunset. These times of day soften shadows and bring out the natural colors in adobe buildings, landscapes, and mountain views.

Highlight Cultural Details

Look for Native American textiles, crafts, and traditional art. Visit local markets and photograph artists at work to capture the city's cultural richness. For a unique perspective, ask artisans about the meaning behind their designs and traditions.

Street Photography at the Railyard

The Railyard District has colorful murals, live music, and bustling markets, perfect for vibrant street shots. This area is where Santa Fe's contemporary vibe shines, with a mix of locals and visitors creating an energetic atmosphere.

Document Local Festivals

Santa Fe's events, such as the Indian Market or Fiesta de Santa Fe, offer prime opportunities for candid shots of dancers, artists, and colorful regalia. Be mindful of cultural etiquette, especially when photographing traditional dances or ceremonies.

Capture the Desert Landscapes

Take advantage of Santa Fe's high-altitude desert to capture striking landscapes. The Sangre de Cristo Mountains, Rio Grande Gorge, and areas around Ghost Ranch offer endless photo opportunities.

Experiment with Light

Santa Fe's sunlight can be harsh during the day, so adjust your camera settings accordingly. Use filters to soften direct sunlight, and try black-and-white photography for a timeless feel on bright, sunny days.

Seasonal Shots

Each season offers unique photographic opportunities in Santa Fe. In spring, capture blooming gardens; in fall, the golden aspens; and in winter, snow-covered adobe buildings. Return in different seasons to document the city's transformations.

Get Close to the Cuisine

Santa Fe's culinary scene is visually stunning. Photograph dishes like blue corn enchiladas, green chile stew, and tamales. Take time to compose your shots and capture the textures, colors, and ambiance of local restaurants.

Explore Hidden Gems and Local Cafes

Local cafes and hidden courtyards often provide charming settings for photos. Stop by tucked-away spots like Op.Cit Books or the patio at La Choza to discover unexpected gems.

Respect Cultural Etiquette

At Pueblo events or sacred sites, ask permission before taking photos, and be aware of any photography restrictions. Respect for these spaces enhances your experience and leaves a positive impression on the community.

Santa Fe provides a variety of photographic opportunities, from expansive landscapes to intricate cultural details. Embrace the city's unique lighting, explore both popular and hidden spots, and adapt to the high desert conditions. By taking the time to frame your shots thoughtfully, you'll create a visual story that captures the heart of the "City Different."

CHAPTER 18

CURATED ITINERARIES FOR EVERY TRAVELER

Santa Fe's rich blend of art, culture, history, and natural beauty provides endless possibilities for exploration. Whether you're visiting for a few days or a couple of weeks, these thoughtfully crafted itineraries are designed to cater to a wide range of interests, including first-time visitors, art lovers, families, adventure seekers, and those with a deep curiosity about the City Different. The personalization of these itineraries ensures that your unique interests and preferences are valued and catered to, making your Santa Fe experience truly special.

3-DAY ITINERARY FOR FIRST-TIME VISITORS

- **Day 1: Cultural Exploration and Historic Plaza District**
  - **Morning**: Start at the **Historic Plaza** to soak in the adobe architecture, visit the **Cathedral Basilica of St. Francis of Assisi**, and explore local shops.
  - **Afternoon**: Lunch at **Cafe Pasqual's**. Then, dive into the art world at the **Georgia O'Keeffe Museum** before heading to **Canyon Road** to explore its many art galleries.

- **Evening**: Dine in the **Railyard Arts District** and, if you're up for it, catch a live performance at **The Lensic** or a local venue.
- **Day 2: Outdoor Adventures and History**
  - **Morning**: Hike to the **Cross of the Martyrs** for panoramic views of Santa Fe, then enjoy breakfast at **Clafoutis**.
  - **Afternoon**: Head to **Bandelier National Monument** for a walk through ancient cliff dwellings and petroglyphs. Enjoy lunch in **Los Alamos**.
  - **Evening**: Return to Santa Fe for dinner at **La Choza** for authentic New Mexican cuisine.
- **Day 3: Culinary Delights and Local Markets**
  - **Morning**: Visit the **Santa Fe Farmers' Market** to savor fresh produce and handmade crafts.
  - **Afternoon**: Take a cooking class at the **Santa Fe School of Cooking**.
  - **Evening**: Wrap up your Santa Fe experience with dinner at **Geronimo** for a fine dining experience.

5-DAY IMMERSIVE SANTA FE EXPERIENCE

- **Days 1-3**: Follow the **3-Day Itinerary** above for a thorough introduction to Santa Fe.
- **Day 4: Day Trip to Taos**
  - **Morning**: Take a scenic drive to **Taos**. Visit **Taos Pueblo**, a UNESCO World Heritage Site.
  - **Afternoon**: Lunch at **Michael's Kitchen** in Taos, then explore the historic Taos Plaza and **Millicent Rogers Museum**.
  - **Evening**: Return to Santa Fe for dinner at **Restaurant Martín**.
- **Day 5: Wellness and Art Exploration**
  - **Morning**: Start with a relaxing spa day at **Ten Thousand Waves**.

- **Afternoon**: Lunch at **Izanami** at the spa, followed by an afternoon exploring more of Santa Fe's art scene in the **Railyard Arts District**.
- **Evening**: Enjoy a farewell dinner at **Sazón** for a taste of elevated Southwestern cuisine.

7-DAY IN-DEPTH SANTA FE JOURNEY

- **Days 1-5**: Follow the **5-Day Itinerary** above for an enriching Santa Fe experience.
- **Day 6: Adventure and Local History**
  - **Morning**: Mountain biking on the **La Tierra Trails** or whitewater rafting on the **Rio Grande** for some adventure.
  - **Afternoon**: Lunch at **Second Street Brewery** and explore the **Baca Street Arts District**.
  - **Evening**: Dinner at **El Farol** with a Flamenco show.
- **Day 7: Museum Exploration and Local Farewell**
  - **Morning**: Visit the **Museum of International Folk Art** and the **Museum of Indian Arts & Culture**.
  - **Afternoon**: Lunch at **SantaCafe** and stroll around the **Santa Fe Botanical Garden**.
  - **Evening**: Conclude with dinner at **The Compound** on Canyon Road.

3-DAY FAMILY FUN ITINERARY WITH SMALL CHILDREN

- **Day 1**: Start at the **Santa Fe Children's Museum** with interactive exhibits perfect for toddlers. **Lunch at Tomasita's** and an afternoon stroll at **Railyard Park** with play areas.
- **Day 2**: Visit the **Harrell House Bug Museum** for fun insect encounters. **Lunch at Plaza Cafe** and explore **Randall Davey Audubon Center** for a gentle nature walk.

- **Day 3**: Morning visit to the **Botanical Garden** for sensory exploration, **lunch at Back Road Pizza**, and a **Meow Wolf** adventure in the afternoon for colorful, sensory stimulation.

OUTDOOR ADVENTURE ITINERARY (3 DAYS)

- **Day 1**: **Morning hike** on the **Dale Ball Trails** followed by a **scenic drive along the Turquoise Trail** with lunch in **Madrid**. Afternoon visit to the **Sangre de Cristo Mountains**.
- **Day 2**: Day trip to **Bandelier National Monument** for hiking and exploration, with lunch at the **Pig + Fig Café** in White Rock.
- **Day 3**: **Whitewater rafting on the Rio Grande** in the morning and a mountain biking session on **La Cuchara Trail** in the afternoon.

ART LOVERS ITINERARY (5 DAYS)

- **Day 1**: Morning in **Canyon Road** galleries, lunch at **Tea House**, and an afternoon at the **Georgia O'Keeffe Museum**.
- **Day 2**: Visit **SITE Santa Fe** and the **Museum of International Folk Art**.
- **Day 3**: Drive to **Taos** to visit the **Millicent Rogers Museum** and explore the Taos art scene.
- **Day 4**: Spend time at **El Museo Cultural de Santa Fe** and end the day at **Santa Fe Playhouse** for a theater performance.
- **Day 5**: Full day of gallery hopping in **Railyard Arts District**, wrapping up with a performance at **The Lensic**.

WELLNESS AND RELAXATION ITINERARY (5 DAYS)

- **Day 1**: Start with a relaxing day at **Ojo Santa Fe Spa Resort**, with lunch on-site.

- **Day 2**: Morning yoga session and afternoon meditation class at **Santa Fe Soul Center for Optimal Health**.
- **Day 3**: Take a **sunset hot air balloon ride** and relax with a sunset picnic.
- **Day 4**: A day at **Ten Thousand Waves** with spa treatments and lunch at **Izanami**.
- **Day 5**: Conclude with a sound bath session and wellness workshop in **Santa Fe Healing Arts Center**.

14-Day Itinerary for Extended Stays

- **Days 1-5**: Follow the **5-Day Immersive Itinerary** for cultural immersion and relaxation.
- **Days 6-7**: Add the **Outdoor Adventure** days, with visits to **Dale Ball Trails**, **Bandelier**, and the **Rio Grande**.
- **Days 8-10**: Integrate the **Art Lovers Itinerary** with Canyon Road and Railyard District explorations.
- **Days 11-12**: Spend a couple of days exploring local neighborhoods such as the **Historic Plaza**, **Canyon Road**, and **Railyard Arts District**.
- **Days 13-14**: Include wellness activities with a day at **Ojo Santa Fe** and a yoga retreat. Conclude with a culinary farewell, visiting **Santa Fe Farmers' Market**, cooking classes, and dining at **Coyote Cafe**.

Each itinerary offers unique insights into Santa Fe's culture, history, and community. Customize your experience by following one or blending a few together to create your perfect Santa Fe adventure.

CONCLUSION

Santa Fe beckons with its distinctive charm and cultural richness in the heart of the American Southwest. The city's unique cultural offerings, from the enchanting Historic Plaza District to the vibrant Railyard Arts District, create a rich array of experiences that are sure to intrigue and inspire those who seek something extraordinary. Santa Fe invites exploration at every turn, promising a journey filled with unique cultural insights.

Each season, Santa Fe undergoes a transformative journey, offering a fresh and exciting perspective. The annual events calendar, adorned with highlights like the Santa Fe Indian Market and the Farolito Walk on Canyon Road, celebrates its diverse heritage and provides immersive experiences for all. The Santa Fe Restaurant Week is a culinary adventure, while the Film Festival offers a chance to engage with the city's cinematic brilliance. Whether you're exploring the art galleries of Canyon Road or savoring live music at the Santa Fe Bandstand, each visit unfolds a unique chapter in the city's dynamic and ever-changing story.

As you read through these pages, you've been introduced to Santa Fe's treasures, yet the real magic lies beyond the words. Venture into lesser-known neighborhoods, connect with locals and embrace spontaneous moments that turn into cherished memories. This city extends beyond its museums and markets—immerse yourself in impromptu performances, local cafes, and the warm hospitality that defines the heart of Santa Fe.

Santa Fe, the City Different, invites you to experience a harmonious blend of tradition and innovation. As adobe walls stand testament to centuries of history, contemporary creativity breathes life into its streets. Whether indulging in culinary delights, discovering neighborhood gems, or participating in the many festivities, Santa Fe will leave an indelible mark on your journey. This city's vibrant hues and cultural notes will forever resonate within you, inviting you back to explore more of its depths.

As we reach the conclusion of this guide, I want to thank you for taking this journey through Santa Fe's streets, savoring its flavors, and uncovering its many facets. I hope that each page has deepened your connection to the City Different and that you leave inspired to explore more. Please consider sharing your thoughts by leaving a review on Amazon. Your honest feedback helps future readers and supports the community that values meaningful travel experiences.

As you close this book, may the memories of Santa Fe stay with you, woven into the fabric of your travel memories, inspiring future adventures in the City Different and beyond. Remember, there's always more to see, and Santa Fe's magic eagerly awaits your return to welcome you back for more exploration.

Thank you for being part of this journey. Your story, like mine, is now intertwined with Santa Fe's. I look forward to seeing how your own journey unfolds in this vibrant, timeless city.

REFERENCES

ARTS AND CULTURE:

- Canyon Road Arts – the complete visitors guide to arts, dining, and the Santa Fe lifestyle. (2016, June 23). Retrieved January 5, 2024, from https://canyonroadarts.com/
- El Rancho de las Golondrinas. (n.d.). Retrieved January 5, 2024, from https://golondrinas.org/
- Museum of International Folk Art. (n.d.). Retrieved January 5, 2024, from https://www.internationalfolkart.org/
- Santa Fe Indian Market | Southwestern Association for Indian Arts (SWAIA). (n.d.). Retrieved January 5, 2024, from https://swaia.org/
- The Georgia O'Keeffe Museum. (2024, January 5). Retrieved January 5, 2024, from https://www.okeeffemuseum.org/
- Welcome to the Wheelwright Museum of the American Indian. (n.d.). Retrieved January 5, 2024, from https://wheelwright.org/

EVENTS AND COMMUNITY RESOURCES:

- Albuquerque International Balloon Fiesta. (n.d.). Retrieved January 5, 2024, from https://www.balloonfiesta.com/
- Santa Fe Bandstand. (n.d.). Retrieved January 5, 2024, from https://santafebandstand.org/
- Santa Fe Farmers' Market Institute. (n.d.). Retrieved January 5, 2024, from https://farmersmarketinstitute.org/
- Santa Fe Independent Film Festival. (n.d.). Retrieved January 5, 2024, from https://santafeindependentfilmfestival.com/
- Santa Fe Wine & Chile Fiesta. (n.d.). Retrieved January 5, 2024, from https://santafewineandchile.org/

HISTORY AND HERITAGE:

- New Mexico History Museum. (n.d.). Retrieved January 5, 2024, from http://nmhistorymuseum.org/
- The Santa Fe Trail Association. (n.d.). Retrieved January 5, 2024, from https://santafetrail.org/

REFERENCES

- True West Magazine: American History and Heritage. (n.d.). Retrieved January 5, 2024, from https://truewestmagazine.com/

LOCAL PUBLICATIONS AND MEDIA:

- New Mexico Magazine. (n.d.). Retrieved January 5, 2024, from https://www.newmexicomagazine.org/
- Pasatiempo – Arts and Culture Weekly. (n.d.). Retrieved January 5, 2024, from https://www.santafenewmexican.com/pasatiempo/
- Santa Fe New Mexican | Santa Fe New Mexico daily news, sports, arts & culture news. (n.d.). Retrieved January 5, 2024, from https://www.santafenewmexican.com/
- The Santa Fe Reporter. (n.d.). Retrieved January 5, 2024, from https://www.sfreporter.com/

OUTDOOR ACTIVITIES AND RECREATION:

- AllTrails – Explore Santa Fe Hiking Trails. (n.d.). Retrieved January 5, 2024, from https://www.alltrails.com/us/new-mexico/santa-fe
- New Mexico Department of Game and Fish. (n.d.). Retrieved January 5, 2024, from https://www.wildlife.state.nm.us/
- Ski Santa Fe. (2023, December 27). Retrieved January 5, 2024, from https://skisantafe.com/
- Turquoise Trail National Scenic Byway. (n.d.). Retrieved January 5, 2024, from https://www.turquoisetrail.org/

DINING AND CULINARY RESOURCES:

- Santa Fe School of Cooking. (n.d.). Retrieved January 5, 2024, from https://santafeschoolofcooking.com/
- Kakawa Chocolate House. (n.d.). Retrieved January 5, 2024, from https://kakawachocolates.com/
- Eater – Santa Fe. (n.d.). Retrieved January 5, 2024, from https://www.eater.com/santa-fe

ADDITIONAL LOCAL ORGANIZATIONS AND SERVICES:

- Meow Wolf: Immersive Art Experiences. (n.d.). Retrieved January 5, 2024, from https://meowwolf.com/
- Santa Fe Botanical Garden. (n.d.). Retrieved January 5, 2024, from https://www.santafebotanicalgarden.org/

REFERENCES

- Santa Fe Institute. (n.d.). Retrieved January 5, 2024, from https://www.santafe.edu/
- Santa Fe Opera. (n.d.). Retrieved January 5, 2024, from https://www.santafeopera.org/
- Santa Fe Railyard. (2023, March 31). Retrieved January 5, 2024, from https://www.railyardsantafe.com/
- TOURISM Santa Fe. (n.d.). Retrieved January 5, 2024, from https://www.santafe.org/

TRAVEL AND VISITOR GUIDES:

- Tripadvisor: Over a billion reviews & contributions for Hotels, Attractions, Restaurants, and more. (n.d.). Retrieved January 5, 2024, from https://www.tripadvisor.com/
- Welcome to Santa Fe New Mexico | City of Santa Fe. (n.d.). Retrieved January 5, 2024, from https://www.santafenm.gov/

ABOUT THE AUTHOR
KIMBERLY BURK CORDOVA

Kimberly Burk Cordova is an accomplished author, entrepreneur, and founder of Cordova Consulting, a multifaceted firm dedicated to leadership development, strategic business solutions, and transformative growth. With over three decades of experience in IT and Technology, Kimberly has built a career marked by innovative projects, leading-edge digital transformations, and a steadfast commitment to fostering personal and professional growth for leaders at all levels. Her expertise, however, extends well beyond the tech world.

A seasoned traveler and cultural enthusiast, Kimberly's adventures span the globe. Her love for exploring diverse histories and immersing herself in other cultures fuels her curiosity and continues to shape her life's work. Now residing in the heart of Santa Fe, New Mexico, Kimberly finds endless inspiration in the city's rich artistic heritage, vibrant cultural scene, and awe-inspiring natural landscapes. Whether capturing the spirit of Santa Fe through her writing or enjoying local music and theater, Kimberly's deep-rooted love for the arts is as vibrant as her passion for travel.

Beyond her professional pursuits, Kimberly embraces the joy and fulfillment of family life. She shares her journey with her husband, Greg, with whom she enjoys the rich cultural diversity of Santa Fe. Kimberly's daughter, Channa, has blessed her with two grandchildren, Vera and Tillman, who bring light and laughter to her days.

Cordova Consulting reflects Kimberly's diverse interests and values. Under its umbrella, she shares her insights on leadership, personal development, and strategic business transformation through books, workshops, and consulting services. The company's publishing arm includes an array of books and resources covering topics like leadership, personal growth, travel, and more. Kimberly's work is not only informative but also immersive, drawing readers into her unique perspective on the world. Her work has had a profound impact on her clients, helping them to achieve their personal and professional goals.

Kimberly's writing style is characterized by her engaging storytelling and her unique ability to weave personal experiences into broader themes. She is more than a writer; she is a storyteller who uses her craft to explore life's richness and invite others to reflect on their own journeys. Whether exploring topics like leadership and resilience or the nuances of global cuisines, she brings warmth, insight, and authenticity to each page, creating a deep connection with her readers.

Join Kimberly on her journey as she continues to uncover the beauty of life's diverse experiences and share her insights with readers and clients alike. Her commitment to growth, learning, and cultural exploration is a testament to her belief in the power of stories to inspire, connect, and transform. We invite you to engage with Kimberly's work and be part of this transformative journey.

amazon.com/author/kimberlycordova

goodreads.com/kbcordova

youtube.com/@CordovaConsulting

facebook.com/CordovaCons

linkedin.com/in/kimberlyburk

tiktok.com/@kimberlyburkcordova

ALSO BY KIMBERLY BURK CORDOVA

LEADERSHIP SERIES

- Turning Chaos into Gold: The Alchemy of Women's Leadership
- The Emotional Intelligence Advantage: Transform Your Life, Relationships, and Career

TRAVEL SERIES

- Santa Fe Uncovered: A Local's Insight into the Heart of New Mexico
- Santa Fe: A Local's Enchanting Journey Through the City Different
- Denver Dossier: Themed Adventures for Every Traveler

EMPOWERING SMALL BUSINESSES SERIES

- Artificial Intelligence Unleashed: An Entrepreneur's Guide to Innovation
- Augmented and Virtual Reality: Unlocking Business Potential for Entrepreneurs

- Cybersecurity for Entrepreneurs: Safeguarding Your Business from Online Threats
- The Entrepreneur's Edge: A 3-Book Compilation on AI, Cybersecurity, and AR/VR

Milton Keynes UK
Ingram Content Group UK Ltd.
UKHW020317021124
450424UK00013B/1297

9 798227 610720